IMAGES
of America

ACWORTH

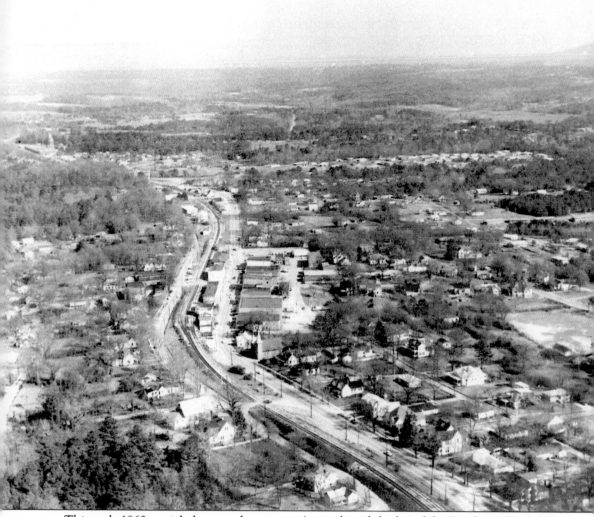

This early 1960s aerial photograph captures Acworth and the lay of the Peachtree Trail, W&A Railroad, the Dixie Highway (also known as Acworth's Main Street), and old U.S. Highway 41. Main Street had been paved in July 1926 with a contract that included convict labor. The most direct Dixie Highway route from the Great Lakes to Florida was completely paved in the fall of 1929. In the height of the vacation season that year, over 800 tourist automobiles were expected daily. During its Dixie Highway heyday, Acworth boasted a Victorian downtown, churches, three textile mills, a chenille toy factory, gas stations, automobile dealers, a tourist court, diners, a bowling alley, a movie theater, and a hotel. The new Highway 41 had bypassed downtown Acworth by the time of this photograph, and the city was just on the cusp of its major suburban growth. (Acworth HPC collection.)

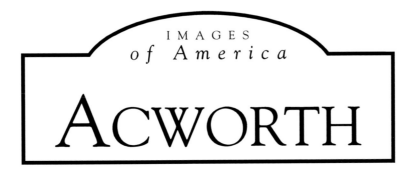

IMAGES
of America

ACWORTH

Acworth Society for Historic Preservation, Inc.

ARCADIA
PUBLISHING

Published by Arcadia Publishing
Charleston, South Carolina

Printed in the United States of America

Library of Congress Catalog Card Number: 2002111297

For all general information contact Arcadia Publishing at:
Telephone 843-853-2070
Fax 843-853-0044
E-mail sales@arcadiapublishing.com
For customer service and orders:
Toll-Free 1-888-313-2665

Visit us on the Internet at www.arcadiapublishing.com

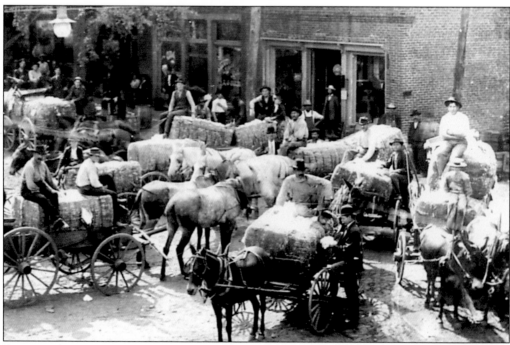

Because of its cotton gins, warehouses, and railway connections, Acworth was a regional center for farmers' crops as evidenced by this 1895 photograph taken at the corner of Main and Dallas Streets. (Acworth HPC collection.)

CONTENTS

ACKNOWLEDGMENTS

The authors want to extend our deepest thanks to Kenneth Parrott for his technical expertise in digital editing of the photographs. We could not have completed this book without his skills and support.

We would also like to thank the following for their assistance in gathering photographs and materials, and for contributing history and background information: City of Acworth Historic Preservation Commission (HPC); Acworth Society for Historic Preservation (ASHP); Silena Jumper; Mark Lemon; Center for Regional Culture and History, Kennesaw State University; and Thomas A. Scott, Ph.D.

Finally, we would like to acknowledge Boyd Parks, Jay Honeycutt, and Ed Lackey for their special contributions.

We are deeply indebted to the members of the Carrie Dyer Women's Club, who wrote an excellent account of Acworth in 1976. *Acworth, Georgia: From Cherokee County to Suburbia* is still a valuable source of information regarding the area's history and character. We consider this book to be a companion piece to that chronicle.

Above all else, we would like to thank the many Acworth families who permitted us to review and scan their photographs, postcards, bibles, diaries, and other memorabilia. If we have not used your photographs, we are nonetheless grateful for your contribution to the archives of the Acworth Society for Historic Preservation. This historic pictorial essay is laced with local legend and family lore and would not have been possible without community support.

Valerie Hart Jordan
Amy Gillis Lowry
Abbie Tucker Parks
November 2002

INTRODUCTION

The Acworth community had its beginnings in commerce and transportation. These ingredients combined with its advantageous geography to make the area a desirable place to settle as it changed from Cherokee territory to a railway center to an automobile tourist stop and finally to an Atlanta suburb. Throughout its history, however, Acworth has never lost its small-town charm.

Present-day Acworth Main Street traces the path of the Peachtree Trail, the Cherokee trade route of the late 1700s. The area was part of the Cherokee nation that, at its peak, stretched from north Georgia into the western Carolinas and Virginia, eastern Tennessee and Kentucky, and into northeast Alabama. By the end of the 18th century, white encroachment shrank Cherokee holdings to north Georgia and small areas of Alabama, Tennessee, and North Carolina. The land grab was exacerbated by the 1828 gold strike in the Auraria/Dahlonega area of northeast Georgia. Prospectors and settlers rushed into Cherokee lands. Georgia seized the territory, surveyed the land, and carved out 40-acre gold and 160-acre farm lots that were distributed in the 1832 land lottery. In 1838–1839, the Cherokees were forcibly removed to Oklahoma by federal troops along the "Trail Where We Cried."

The Georgia legislature created Cobb County from the larger Cherokee County in December 1832. The future town of Acworth would be located in extreme northwest Cobb County—30 miles north of Atlanta and 15 miles north of Marietta, the county seat. The settlement would draw trade from neighboring Bartow, Cherokee, and Paulding Counties. Pioneer families settling in the Acworth area included Lemon, Awtrey, McMillan, Collins, Stokely, Pitner, Scroggs, Mitchell, Eccles, Baker, Priest, Prichard, Smith, Northcutt, Davenport, Orr, and Cowan/Cowen. The terrain, on the southern edge of the Appalachian Mountains and well served by numerous creeks, was suited to subsistence farming and cotton growing. There were also small amounts of gold in the area from the large vein running southwest from Dahlonega. Gold was reportedly found in nearby creeks, including Proctor, Allatoona, and the aptly-named Gold.

The frontier was soon connected to established towns via the Western and Atlantic Railroad that was to run from Marthasville (later renamed Atlanta) to Chattanooga, Tennessee. In the late 1830s, the W&A Railroad was surveyed much along the same route as the Peachtree Trail to the Allatoona Mountains just north of Acworth. By the early 1840s, the rail line was completed as far north as Acworth and a water stop, Northcutt Station (named for railroad agent Alexander Northcutt), was established there. The W&A Railroad thus determined the siting of the town

7

as newcomers settled near the tracks.[1] Joseph Gregg, a local railroad engineer, renamed the small settlement in 1843 for his hometown in Acworth, New Hampshire. By the late 1840s Acworth was "a small village . . . in the midst of a thickly settled country" with a population of 50.[2] On December 1, 1860—the eve of the Civil War—the town was incorporated with its limits extending in a half-mile radius from the W&A Depot at Main and Lemon Streets.

Acworth and her railroad played an important role in the Civil War. Both the Union and Confederate forces fought for control of the tracks from Chattanooga to Atlanta for strategic and supply purposes. In early June of 1864, Union Gen. William T. Sherman and his troops camped in Acworth. The area witnessed minor skirmishes and major battles within a few miles: New Hope Church on May 25, Pickett's Mill on May 27, Dallas on May 28, and Kennesaw Mountain on June 27. Acworth homes and churches served as field headquarters and hospitals. After the capture of Atlanta, Acworth witnessed its closest action in the Battle of Allatoona Pass on October 5. On November 13, 1864, Sherman's troops burned much of Acworth, leaving fewer than a dozen structures, as they set off on their march to the sea. Acworth families scattered; farms and businesses were shattered.

After the difficult Reconstruction years, Acworth began her recovery. The value of farmlands doubled between 1870 and 1890, although by the turn of the century half of those farming were tenants rather than owners.[3] The town boasted two flour mills and a tannery. It was a regional center for cotton warehousing, ginning, and transport. The cotton economy propelled the growth of Acworth's commercial district. In 1880 Acworth reportedly shipped 6,000 cotton bales annually, along with large quantities of dried fruit, flour, and leather, while several highly valued gold mines in the vicinity paid satisfactory dividends.[4]

With the scourge of bad weather and the boll weevil in the late 1910s and early 1920s, the city attempted to diversify the cotton economy. Acworth aggressively pursued industrial growth. The Acworth Board of Trade was established in 1907 to advance the economy. In the 1920s the city advertised for new residents, businesses, and tourists and offered city and county tax exemptions for five years to new industries. Acworth touted its rail and Dixie Highway connections and its close proximity to major markets. A city booster wrote in 1929, "Acworth wants you to make your home here . . . if you are no drone and are honest."[5] By this time, Acworth had three major textile mills employing hundreds of workers.

Following on the heels of the cotton bust, the Great Depression of the 1930s was another setback that hampered the city's growth. The economic surge of World War II was a jumpstart. Bell Aircraft Corporation's Marietta plant transformed Cobb County into an industrial center as B-29s began to roll off the assembly line. Many Acworthians began the daily trek down the Dixie Highway to their factory jobs. In the 1940s and 1950s, Acworth began the transition from small town to suburban community, with newcomers settling in town and commuting to jobs in Marietta and Atlanta. With the completion of Lakes Allatoona and Acworth—Army Corps of Engineers projects harnessing hydroelectric power and impounding drinking water—Acworth itself became a recreation destination for Atlanta-area residents in the 1950s.

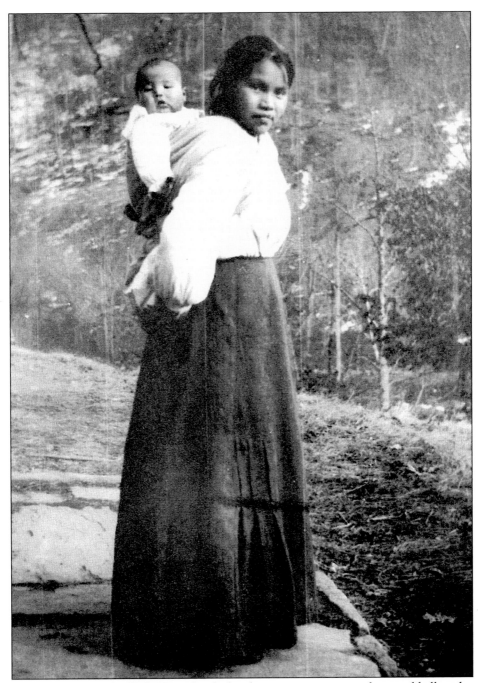

The Cherokee under Chief John Ross fought hard to negotiate a treaty that would allow them to remain in their homes and villages. Although the Supreme Court ruled that the state of Georgia had no jurisdiction over Cherokee lands, President Andrew Jackson would not intervene in the unlawful territory seizure. The Cherokee were eventually dragged out of their dwellings by force with only the clothes on their backs. Those who refused to move to Oklahoma escaped into North Carolina's Blue Ridge Mountains. Some, like this turn-of-the-19th-century Cherokee woman, would inhabit ancestral lands.[6] (Silena Jumper collection.)

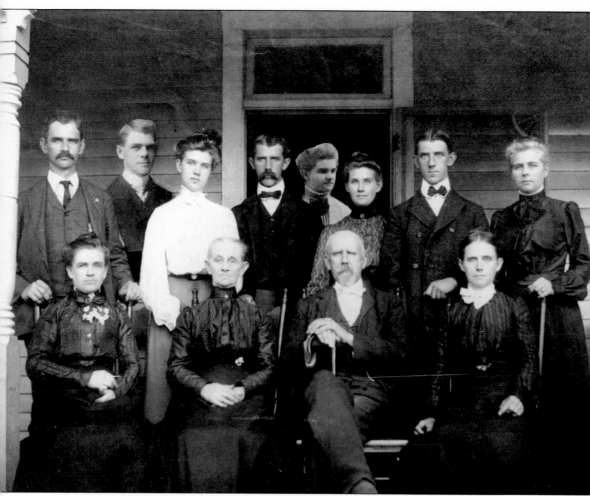

After the death of James Lemon in 1849, his grown son Smith (1821–1889) and 14-year-old son James Lile (1835–1907) took over support of the family, with James Lile eventually joining his brother in his various businesses. The brothers were instrumental in helping to rebuild an Acworth ravaged by the Civil War. Smith soon reopened his S. Lemon Banking Company. James Lile served as bank president, city alderman, and a church elder in the Acworth Presbyterian Church. In this 1906 photograph, James Lile and Eliza Jane Davenport (1837–1916) Lemon posed for their 50th wedding anniversary on the porch of their home with their 10 children. From left to right are (front row) Emma Alice Lemon McMillan, Eliza, James Lile, and Mariah Lemon Nichols; (back row) George, James, Mae Lemon Smith, Edward, Alva Lemon Tapp, Jennie, Clayton "Clate," and Mollie Lemon Pritchard. James and Alva may not have been available for the portrait; their likenesses have been added to the second row by the photographer at a later date. James Lile died the year after this photograph was taken. (Mark Lemon collection.)

One

PIONEER FAMILIES

Starting in the 1830s, pioneer families came to the Acworth area to farm, typically migrating from elsewhere in Georgia or from the Carolinas. Agricultural practices of the day depleted the soil and farmers moved on to newly opened lands. A few prospectors also arrived to try their luck at mining or panning the area creeks. Most yeoman farmers worked their own land; some used slaves as field and domestic workers. In 1851 there were 96 slaves owned by 33 residents of northwest Cobb County; no one held more than ten slaves and the average was three.[7] Farms were small but as Acworth's commerce developed, surplus produce could be sold in town.

By the second or third generation many of the pioneer descendants were in trades or in-town businesses that served the surrounding farmland. An 1883 resident and business directory[8] cites the city population at 500 and lists 128 businessmen, heads of family, widows, and unmarried women living in town. The occupations provided the full range of services to an agrarian community: farmers, clerks, merchants, mechanics, saddlers, blacksmiths, tanners, butchers, shoemakers, carpenters, teachers, railroad agents, doctors, and lawyers. Of the residents listed, 24 are African-American men and women who worked as laborers, carpenters, shoemakers, blacksmiths, waiters, servants, and cooks.

James and Mary Lemon moved from Decatur in DeKalb County to Cobb in 1843 and to Acworth in 1845. James was a wounded War of 1812 veteran and had held elective offices in DeKalb County. The Lemons and their descendants would contribute much to Acworth's development.

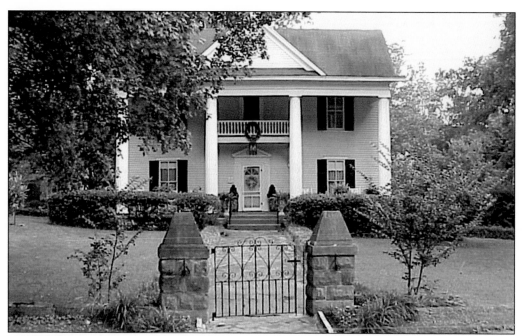

James and Mary Lemon purchased 800 acres of land near the town center and built a small frame house. Shortly before his 1856 marriage, their son James Lile expanded the dwelling into a Carolina-style, modified Plantation Plain house. The Lemon house was remodeled in the 1890s and the two-story front porch was replaced with the neoclassical Doric colonnade as evidenced in this present-day photograph. (Photo by Kenneth Parrott.)

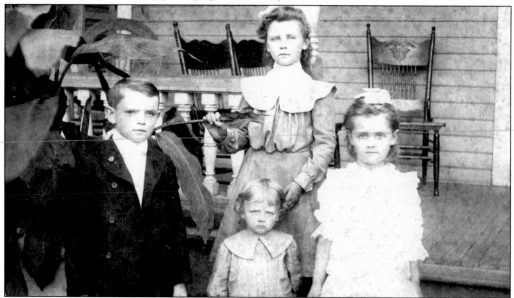

The children of George and Louise Lemon posed on the steps of the Lemon house on Willis Street in 1906. Pictured from left to right are Elvin Lee, Odessa, John Quincy, and Fannie Mae. After the deaths of James Lile and Eliza, the home was purchased by their eldest daughter Mariah and her husband John Nichols. The house passed from family hands in 1975 but since 1993 has been occupied by direct descendants. (Mark Lemon collection.)

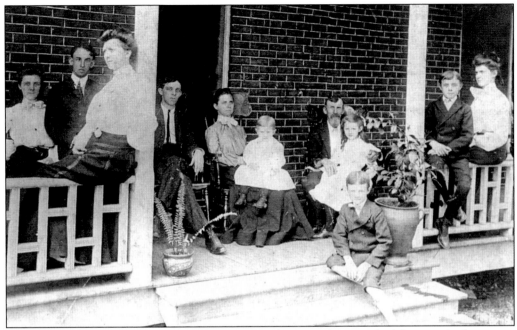

Mariah Lemon married John Nichols in 1879. They are photographed here with their nine children on the porch of a Nichols home that no longer exists. John had a varied career as a horse trader, realtor, stockyard owner, livery stable proprietor, and ice deliverer. Like Eliza's parents, the Nichols lived to celebrate their 50th wedding anniversary. (Mark Lemon collection.)

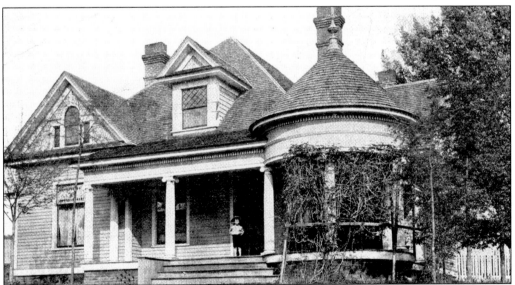

Edward W. Lemon built a classic Queen Anne house on Lemon Street in 1900. This 1910 postcard shows the residence with its wrap-around, turreted porch and columns complemented by Greek Ionic capitals. Other distinctive facade features are asymmetrical placement of dormers, windows, and doors; decorative shingles; and stained glass. The house remains little changed today; even the wisteria visible here still grows in front of the porch. (Emory and Beverly Noland collection.)

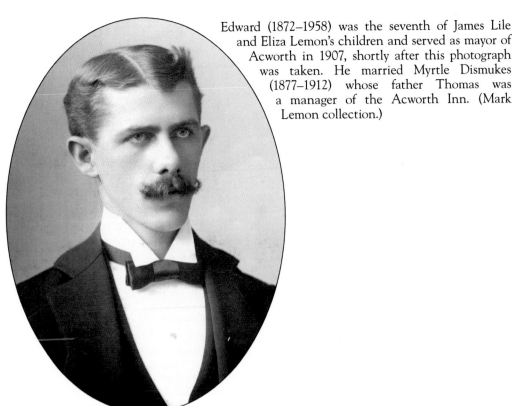

Edward (1872–1958) was the seventh of James Lile and Eliza Lemon's children and served as mayor of Acworth in 1907, shortly after this photograph was taken. He married Myrtle Dismukes (1877–1912) whose father Thomas was a manager of the Acworth Inn. (Mark Lemon collection.)

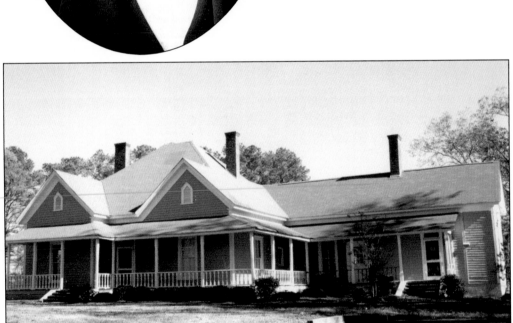

By 1850 Thomas (1802–1897) and Clara (1813–1879) Davenport had moved to a 500-acre farm on Acworth Due West Road. The original homestead was replaced between 1880 and 1900 with the residence as currently shown here. Capt. James Lile Lemon recruited his brothers-in-law, William and Marcus Davenport, sons of Thomas and Clara, to serve in the Confederate Army. Both were killed as they fought side by side during the bloody battle of Antietam. After the war, Captain Lemon dug up their bodies and brought them home. (ASHP collection.)

Four generations of McMillans are captured in this photograph from the early 1880s: Claude (born 1879), father James Wilson "Jim" (1852–1929), grandfather Robert Huie (1829–1907), and great-grandfather George Washington (1805–1887). The patriarch George McMillan acquired a gold lot adjoining Pumpkinvine Creek in the Cherokee land lottery and moved there with his wife Sallie Huie and four children in 1833. George and Sallie were founders of Mars Hill Presbyterian Church. (Nancy McMillan MacPherson collection.)

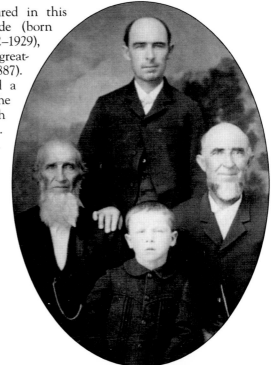

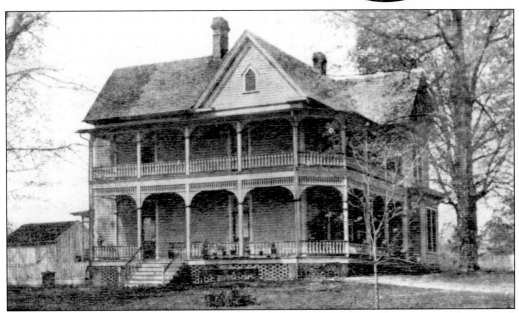

Jim McMillan moved to Acworth from Mars Hill in the 1870s and went into the general merchandise business with his brother-in-law, Jesse Lemon. Jim purchased an existing, two-room antebellum home and five acres of land from the McEver family. Shortly before his 1879 marriage to Emma Alice Lemon (1861–1913), he spent $1500 enlarging the home as shown here and almost an additional $1500 building the porch and decorative gingerbread. (Nancy McMillan MacPherson collection.)

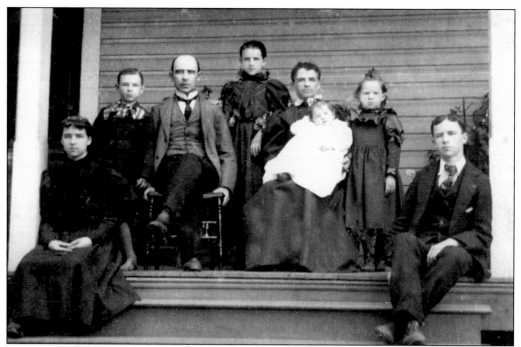

Jim and Emma McMillan were photographed on the front steps of their home in 1896 with six of their ten children. After selling the business venture with Jesse Lemon, Jim formed McMillan Brothers general store with his brother Robert Lee in 1896. He was also a president of the S. Lemon Banking Company. (Nancy McMillan MacPherson collection.)

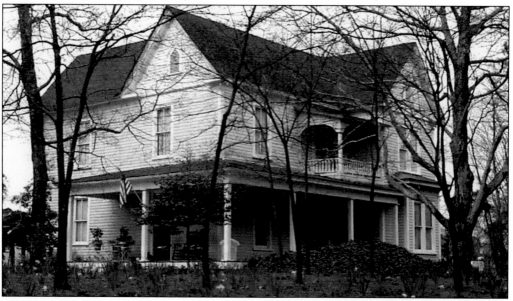

The Jim McMillan home is part of the Collins Avenue Historic District. In 1971 it was sold to Acworth First Baptist Church, whose lot it adjoined on Main Street. In 1980 the home was moved one block north of its original location to Collins Avenue. Only a small portion, a front balcony, remains of the second-story, wrap-around porch as evidenced in this current photograph. (ASHP collection.)

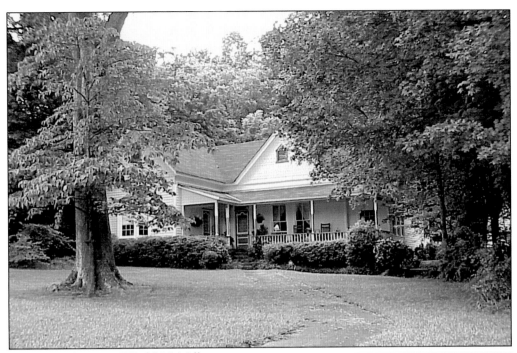

George Washington "Wash" McMillan was Jim's brother. This recent photograph shows the Victorian folk cottage he built in 1891, the year following his marriage to Della Callaway. Wash (1868–1943) was in the livery business with his brother-in-law Richard Carnes, became a cotton buyer, and later had a coal, brick, lime, and cement business for 50 years on North Main Street. He reportedly learned brick making from Smith Lemon. (Photo by Kenneth Parrott.)

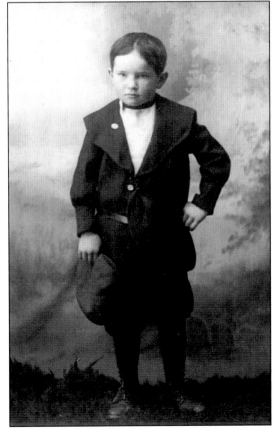

Wash and Della McMillan had three children: Elizabeth "Bess" Callaway (b. 1897), Charles Huie (b. 1901 and pictured here), and Mary Dell (b. 1904). Della died at age 34 in 1905. Wash went on to serve on the Cobb County School Board and as mayor of Acworth from 1923 to 1925 and from 1929 to 1930. (Jane McMillan Baird collection.)

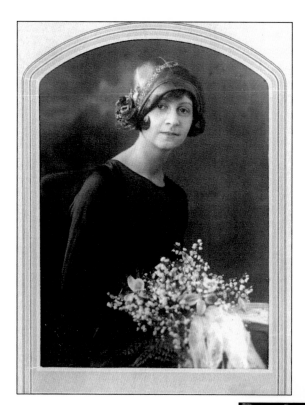

Elizabeth Collins, daughter of C.A. Collins, married Charles Huie McMillan, Wash's son, at the Acworth Baptist Church in 1925. In this bridal portrait, according to the newspaper wedding account, she wore "a cuckoo satin crepe model fashioned on straight lines, with trimmings of darker toned velvet and gold ornaments," and "a small hat of brown satin and gold lace." Her "something old" was a lace handkerchief belonging to her aunt. (Jane McMillan Baird collection.)

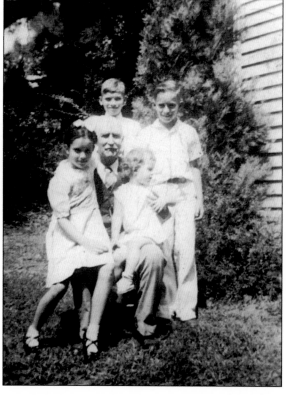

Wash McMillan was photographed in 1940 with his grandchildren through Elizabeth and Charles McMillan and through Mary Dell and Raymond Williams. The children are, from left to right, Jane McMillan, Suzanne McMillan, Ray Williams and Charles Huie McMillan Jr. (Jane McMillan Baird collection.)

Another McMillan brother, Robert Lee "Bob" (1866–1947), married Marie Knox of Kentucky. The first two of their six children, Knox and Elizabeth, are shown in this 1890s photograph. Bob was first a chair maker, then a partner in McMillan Brothers, and later a vice-president and president of the Bank of Acworth. He also served as Acworth mayor and as an alderman. He was instrumental in bringing water and electricity to Acworth. (Nancy McMillan MacPherson collection.)

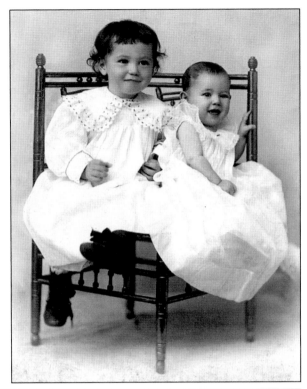

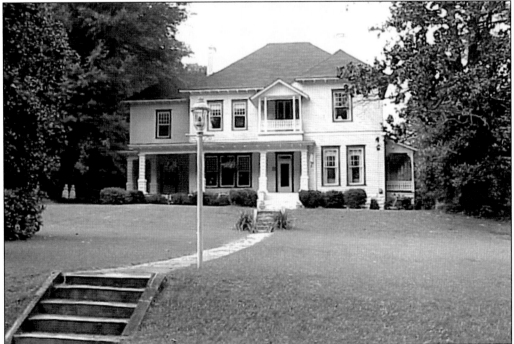

The Bob McMillan home on Northside Drive was built in the early 1900s with architecture influenced by folk Victorian and Craftsman styles as evidenced by this modern photo. Six of the original ten acres of property are still intact. (Photo by Kenneth Parrott.)

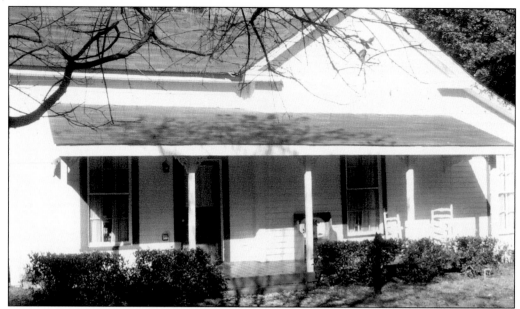

Behind the Bob McMillan home sits an older, simpler cottage. According to local lore, a deaf mute named "Chick" lived here. Chick, a freed slave, used her hands to communicate and lived in the cottage until her death. Until recently, the cottage shown here in a current photograph had no electricity or running water. (Photo by Tommy Allegood.)

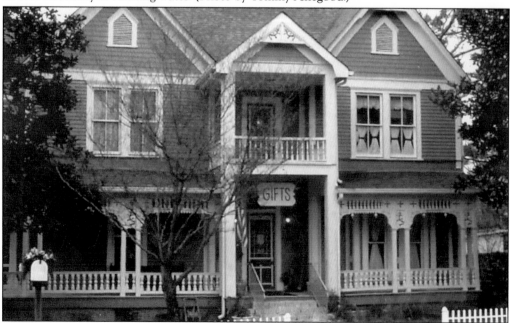

The Jesse L. Lemon House on Main Street was built in the 1880s by Jesse as a wedding gift for his bride, Elizabeth "Lizzie" McMillan, daughter of Robert Huie McMillan. Jesse (1859–1925) was the son of Smith Lemon. He owned a cotton warehouse and a mercantile store, and he served in Acworth's first government after the Civil War. The home's fanciful spindle work and interior staircase featuring carved petit-four laced treads attest to his and the town's prosperity in the Victorian era. (ASHP collection.)

A late 1880s photo shows Orlando (1855–1943) and Belle Awtrey (1861–1903) and four of their ten children. From left to right the children are Raymond Hill, Lemon Merrill, Leone, and Orlando Jr., known as "Gan." Orlando was a prominent merchant and longtime president of the S. Lemon Banking Company. He also served as a city alderman, school board member, and Georgia state representative for three terms. (Reginald Awtrey Collection.)

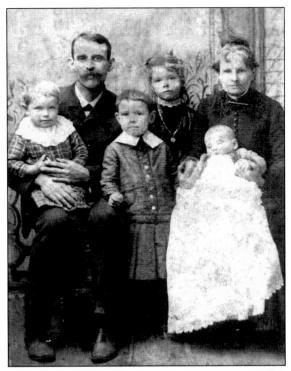

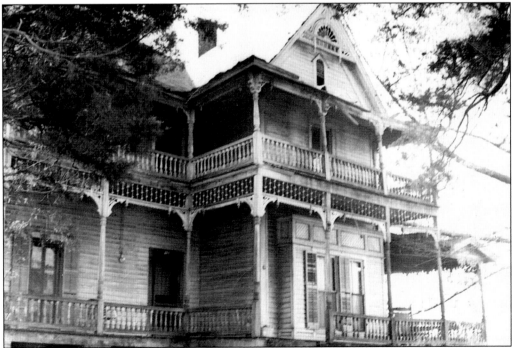

The Orlando Awtrey home was built in 1882 on a 75-acre estate across Dallas Street from the Acworth School. The Awtreys hosted many parties and dances in the gay 1890s and early 1900s in their 10-room Victorian home. The house remained in the family until the 1960s. It was later razed and replaced by a parking lot for Acworth School. (Reginald Awtrey Collection.)

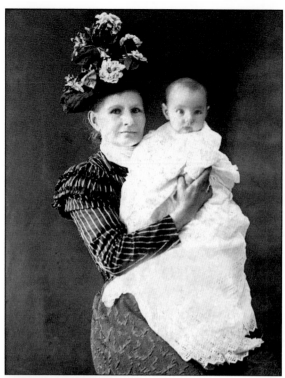

Martha Isabelle "Belle" Lemon Awtrey, a daughter of Smith and Annie Lemon, posed with son Earle in the early 1900s. She died shortly after the photograph was taken at the age of 42. (Reginald Awtrey Collection.)

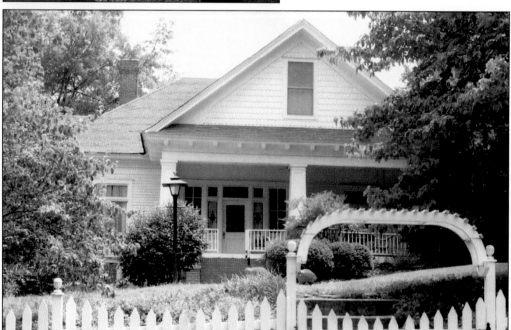

Known as the "Honeymoon House," this large Craftsman bungalow was built on the corner of Dallas Street and Seminole Drive by Lemon Awtrey in 1907 for his bride, Varah Hill. The home contains 13 rooms and 5 bathrooms and features stained glass, decorative shingles and a door with a transom and sidelights. Lemon was a president of the S. Lemon Banking Company, mayor of Acworth in 1918–1919, and a longtime alderman. (ASHP collection.)

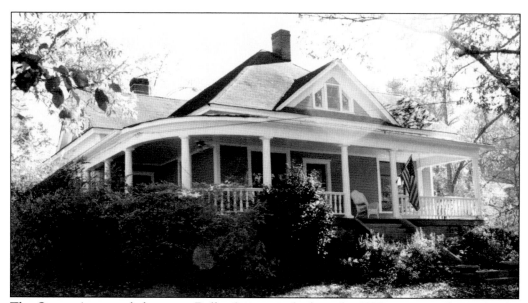

The Queen Anne–style home on Dallas Street was built in the 1890s as a guest house for the Awtrey Estate. The home initially consisted of five rooms on one floor. It has been expanded as evidenced by this view of the home today. The doors, trim, mantles, and stained glass are original. (ASHP collection.)

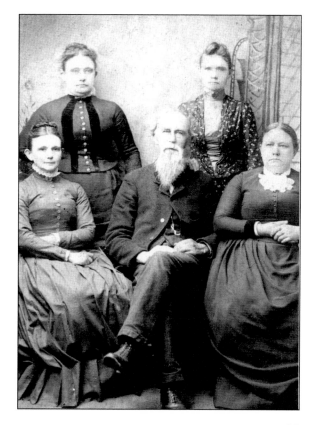

Pioneer citizen Anthony Smith (d. 1895, age 73) is pictured here with his daughters, c. 1880. They are, from left to right, (front row) Sally Barrett and Bettie Quillian; (back row) Jane Smith and Dora Rosa "Rose" Smith. Smith was a founding member of the Acworth Christian Church, but no relation to Rev. Nathan Smith. (Reginald Awtrey Collection.)

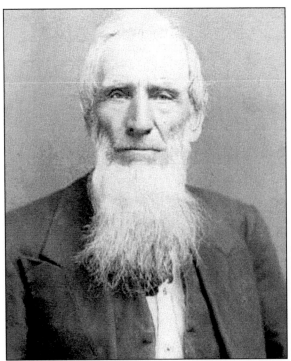

The Rev. Nathan W. Smith (1813–1899) moved to Acworth around 1848. He was one of the first teachers for the fledgling town and a founder of the Acworth Christian Church. He served as its first minister from 1858 to 1864 and again in 1875–1876, helping to rebuild the church after Union soldiers destroyed it. He was also an itinerant preacher, traveling throughout Georgia to promote unity between churches. (Randy Jenkins collection.)

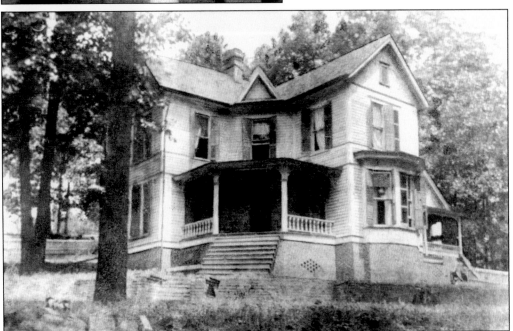

The Mitchell property on today's Southside Drive included the site for the original Christian Church, John Cowan's flour mill, and the city's water tower. The original Robert Morrow Mitchell house photographed here was built in 1892 and burned down in 1911. In 1860 Robert (1836–1903) married Fannie (1840–1925), the Rev. Nathan Smith's daughter. Robert was a C.S.A. Captain in the 23rd Georgia and a wounded veteran. He was a school teacher and served as president of the first Acworth government after the war. (Frances Mitchell Dooley collection.)

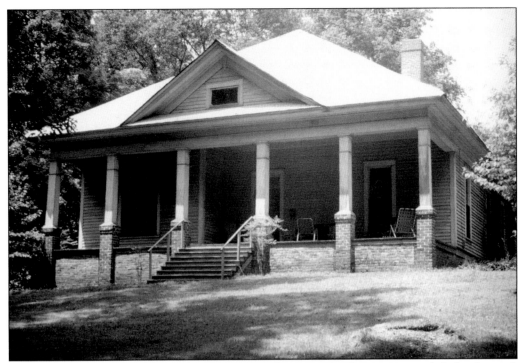

This Mitchell home was built in the 1910s as a replacement for the structure at left that burned. The Mitchells had five children, including son Pendleton "Penn" (1867–1934). Penn married Zula Gunter Ray (1871–1955) in 1889. He and Zula raised their children in both of these homes. (Frances Mitchell Dooley collection.)

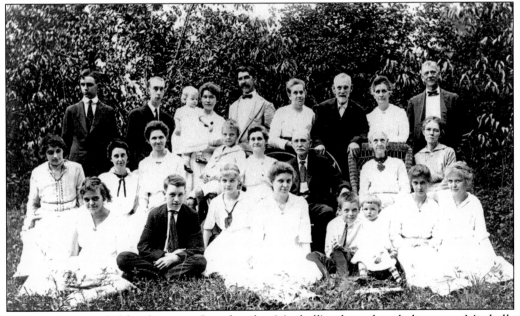

In 1915, the extended family met in Grandmother Mitchell's side yard, including some Mitchells from Texas. Fannie Mitchell is seated in the wicker chair. Penn stands at the far right in the last row; his wife Zula is seated in front of him. (Frances Mitchell Dooley collection.)

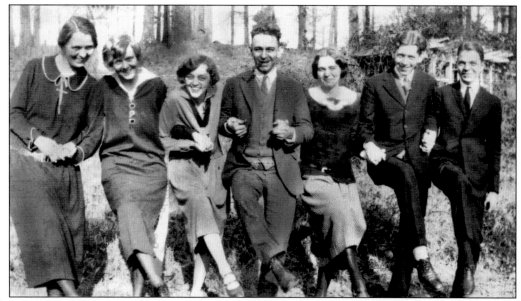

The seven children of Penn and Zula Ray Gunter seem to be enjoying themselves in this image from the 1920s. Pictured from left to right are Lula, Raymer "Zula Ray," Eugenia Small, Robert Morrow "Bob," Dorothy "Dot," Pendleton Jr. "Pent," and Frances. (Frances Mitchell Dooley collection.)

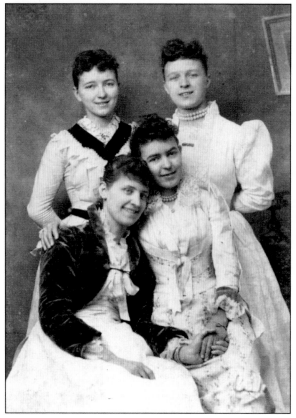

James Crittendon Stokely, son of Acworth farmer D.V. Stokely, was a storeowner, real estate salesman, photographer, and mayor of Acworth. His sisters posed in his studio in this c. 1900 photograph. Seated from left to right are Addie Stokely Beasley and Lydia Stokely Beasley; standing are Helen Stokely Northcutt and Jane "Miss Jennie" Stokely Burnett, a music teacher. (Vanishing Georgia collection, Georgia Dept. of Archives and History.)

Pictured here are William Eccles Orr (1814–1888) and Nancy Green (1822–1899), who were married in Cobb County in 1838. As a young man, William came with his parents, John and Elizabeth Eccles, to settle first near Proctor Creek, then Allatoona Creek. The elder Orrs were two of eight charter members of the Mars Hill Presbyterian Church founded in 1837. (Odene Rakestraw collection.)

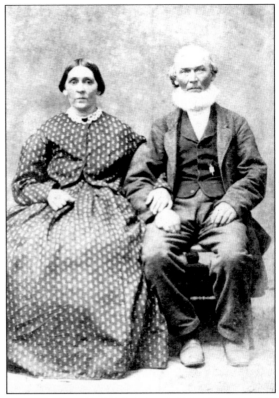

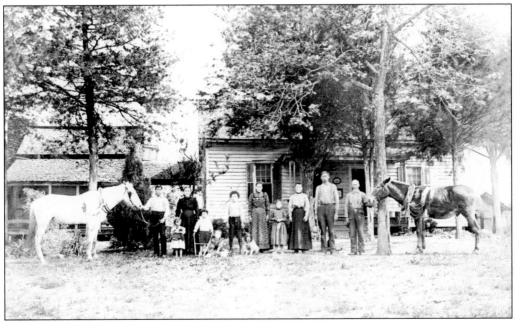

The homeplace of William Eccles Orr was located on Hadaway Road near Acworth Due West Road. The family of Alston Dewitt Green and Elvira Orr Green (William's daughter) stands in front of the house. Pictured from left to right are Judson, Anna, Elvira, George, Minnie, Billy, Dora, Nancy, Fannie, David Dickson (cousin), and Alston. (Odene Rakestraw collection.)

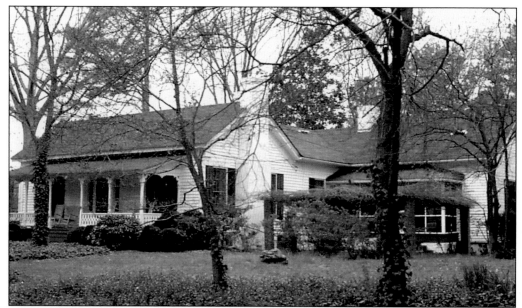

Revolutionary War patriot Capt. John Collins (1760–1852), his wife Phebe Sailors, and son Daniel (1813–1890) settled in Acworth in the 1830s and built this central hallway-style farmhouse atop a small rise. John, Phebe, and Daniel were all founders of the Liberty Hill Baptist Church in 1840. In 1846, Daniel married Isabella Lemon, a sister of Smith and James Lile. They had three sons, including John or J.F. (1852–1924). (ASHP collection.)

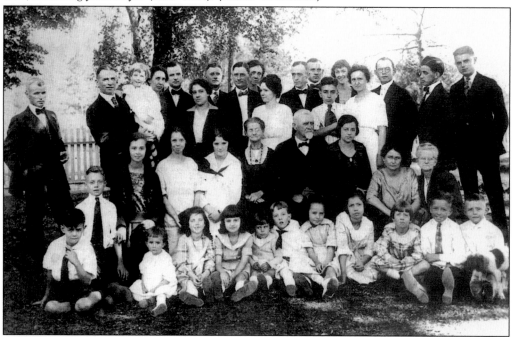

The J.F. and Mary McLain (1850–1932) Collins family was photographed at the homestead on Collins Avenue in the early 1920s. The farm on which the home sat measured over 200 acres and probably extended to present-day Lake Allatoona. The house on Collins Avenue has been modified over time to accommodate family growth. (Acworth HPC collection.)

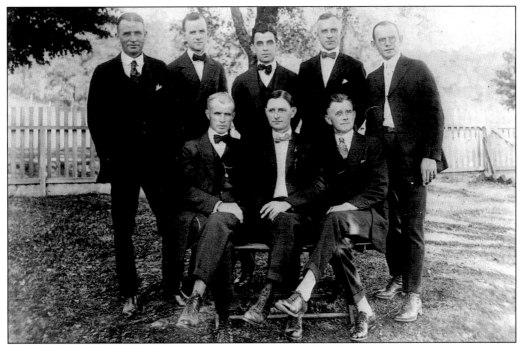

The eight sons of J.F. Collins posed in their yard in the early 1920s. Seated from left to right are Jack, Dee "Judge Daniel," and Cliff; standing are Ernest, Jim, John, Norman, and Roy. J.F. started a furniture store in 1886 on Main Street. From chair and furniture manufacture to special-order casket construction, the business evolved into embalming and funerals by 1898. In 1900 son Ernest followed J.F. into the business. (Acworth HPC collection.)

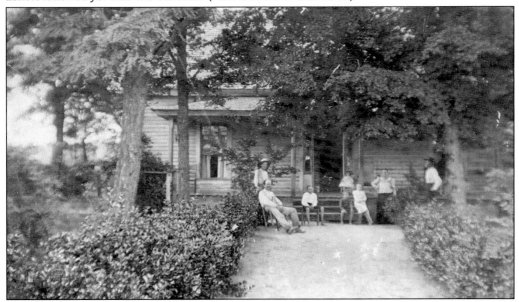

From 1897 to 1912 the McCollum family lived on the property that is now the City of Acworth's Logan Farm Park. Y.D. "Young Daniel," his wife Mary Jane Kitchens, and other McCollum family members are photographed on the porch of the home. The home and about 30 acres of the farm are incorporated into the park. (William and Helen Roberson collection.)

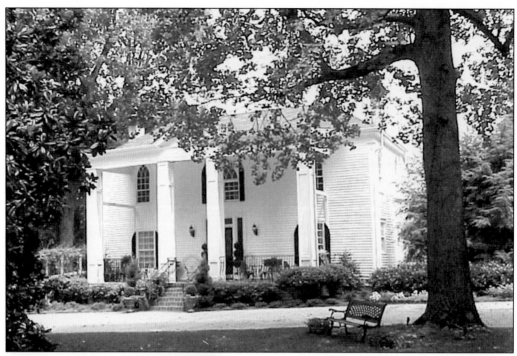

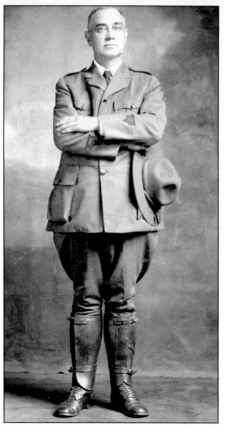

Julia "Bunnie" Cotten (1847–1903) married M. Jack Abbott (1846–1910.) Bunnie was the daughter of Dr. A. Cotten. The Cottens and Jack Abbott moved to Acworth from Powder Springs and were charter members of the Acworth Presbyterian Church. Jack owned a general store in town and served as postmaster for a few years. Their son, Walter Lafayette Abbott (1870–1932), is dressed here in his YMCA uniform. In it he rode the trains during World War I and passed out bibles to soldiers. He was a bookkeeper and a cotton buyer. He married Katherine Phoebe Christian (1871–1947) in 1891. They bought an imposing, white-columned, Greek Revival home (pictured above) on Northside Drive in 1916,pictured above, naming the spacious property "Cedars." (Abbott family collection.)

Katherine Abbott, son William Joseph "Will Jo"(1905–1990), and granddaughter Angela stand in front of Cedars *c*. 1940. Angela's mother, the former Dixie Neal (1913–1993), married Will Jo in 1937. Five generations of Abbotts eventually lived in Cedars. Constructed between 1855 and 1870, the house was known for its windows, Gothic-pointed arches with hood molding, and its beautiful painted ceilings. The Moore family was probably the earliest owner. (Abbott family collection.)

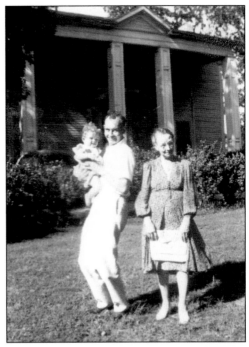

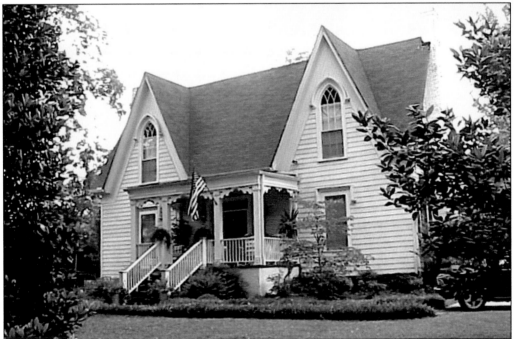

This 1848 Gothic Revival home on Northside Drive was built for and occupied by the Moore family for over a century. The home originally sat on a profitable plantation. It was the only "Pastor's" style house in the area, designed to accommodate itinerant pastors of all denominations. The original back staircase allowed ministers to come and go without disturbing the family. This view today illustrates that the original second-story windows are identical to those in the home at left. (Photo by Kenneth Parrott.)

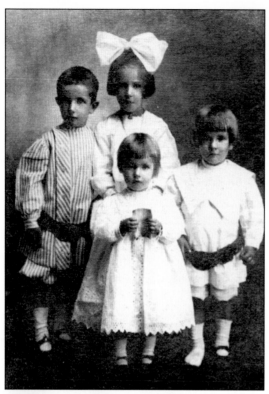

The Parris home place was located on 142 acres on County Line Road in the vicinity of the present-day Brookstone housing development. Bee (1882–1961) and Mamie Parris (1883–1962) farmed and raised their four children on the ancestral land. Bee also worked as a carpenter. The children were photographed c. 1910 in outfits hand made by Mamie. From left to right are Henry B. (b. 1906), Effie Lou (b. 1904), Florence (b. 1908), and Eugene (b. 1908). (Florence Burtz collection.)

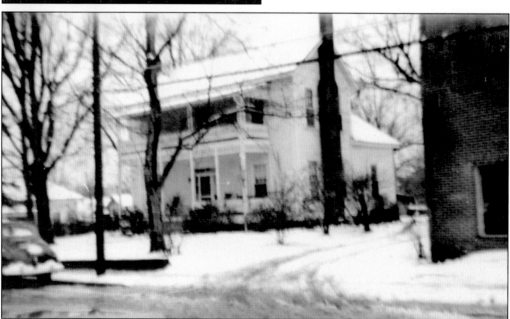

Florence Parris taught school for 35 years, beginning at Allatoona where she had been a student, then at Mars Hill, and finally at Acworth where she had also attended high school, riding a buggy one hour each way. She married Dr. Burtz's son, William, and moved to this Plantation Plain house on Lemon Street that his parents had previously owned. The house is shown here in 1958; later owners added the current brick facade. (Florence Burtz collection.)

Dr. C.W. (1871–1931) and Lizzie West Burtz came to Acworth at the turn of the 19th century from the Crossroads Community that was located in the vicinity of present-day Highways 41 and 92. Their children were also photographed c. 1910. From left to right, they are William (b. 1908), Estelle (b. 1904), and George (b. 1906). (Florence Burtz collection.)

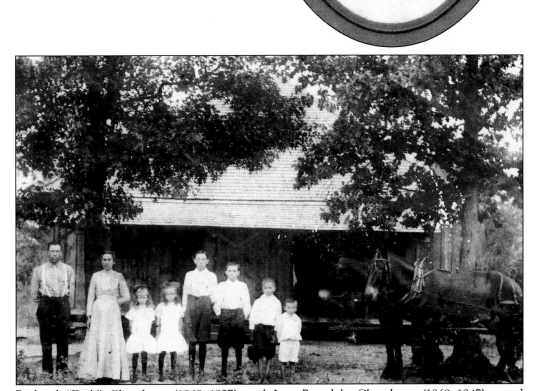

Richard "Dick" Cheatham (1869–1937) and Lou Ragsdale Cheatham (1869–1947) posed with their family—from left to right, twin girls Ethel and Effie, Howard, Virgil Eugene, Clate, and R.A—at the homeplace on present-day Cheatham Road in the early 1900s. (Gene Cheatham collection.)

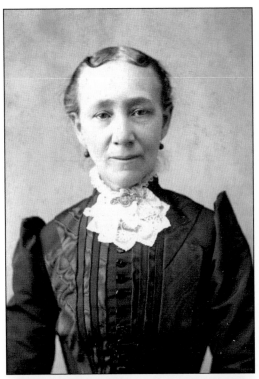

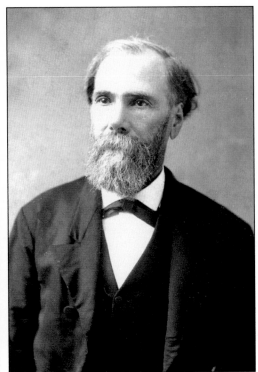

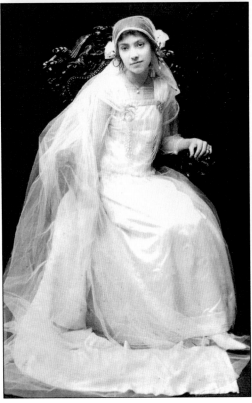

George S. Avery married Mary Ann Gragg in 1858. George had come to Acworth in 1852. The Averys were early members of the Acworth Christian Church and lived in the Plantation Plain–style home still existing on Academy Street at Lakeshore Drive. Fannie Mae Tippin, granddaughter of the Averys through their daughter Ida, was the bride of Carl C. Butler in 1916. She was also one of only two women to serve on the Acworth School Board. Her husband Carl established the Acworth Motor Firm in 1925 and was mayor for ten one-year terms, nine of them consecutive from 1933 to 1941. (Willie B. Kemp collection.)

Master Roy Tippen (1891–1959), grandson of the Averys and son of Sidney J. and Ida Tippen, had his portrait made in J.C. Stokely's photography studio in the early 1890s. Roy Tippen was a railroad telegraph operator and a dairy farmer of registered Jerseys. He married Mamie Lena Bostick, whose parents, John and Annie, ran the Acworth Hotel during World War I. (Willie B. Kemp collection.)

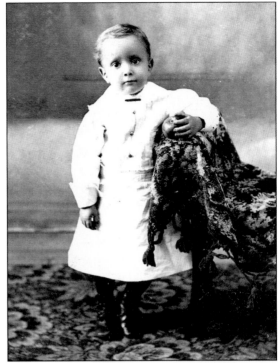

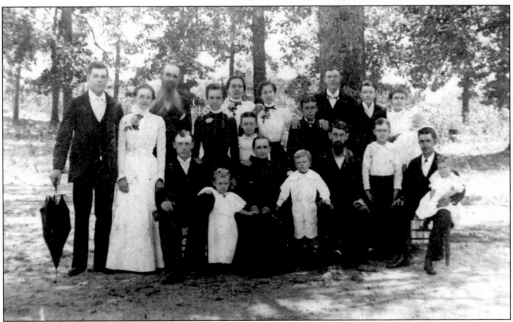

Thomas G. Pitner (1851–1921) and his wife Martha (1852–1906) came to Cobb County from Union City and at one time owned 400 acres of land along Pitner Road from McLain Road to the current county landfill. The Pitner family, pictured here in the early 1900s, included son Marion, a syrup maker, carpenter, and builder of homes on Seminole Drive and son Jim, a blacksmith and father of Harmon, a Bank of Acworth president and a city alderman. (Hinton Brown collection.)

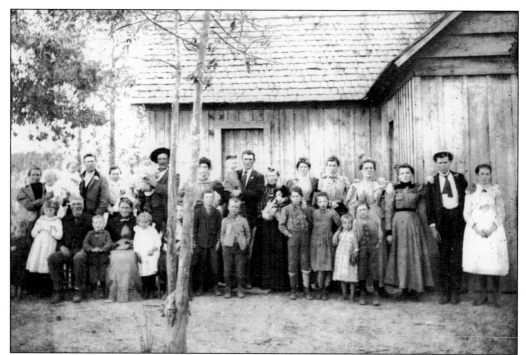

Acworth pioneer Ezra Stephen Baker (1811–1895) and his wife Rebecca (nee Priest, 1820–1898) came to the Acworth area in the 1850s. They sit with their family in this 1890s photograph. The Bakers owned land out Hickory Grove Road near Hickory Grove (formerly Flint Hill) Baptist Church. The Bakers deeded land to deacons of the church for its construction, and they are buried in its graveyard. (Lil Prather collection.)

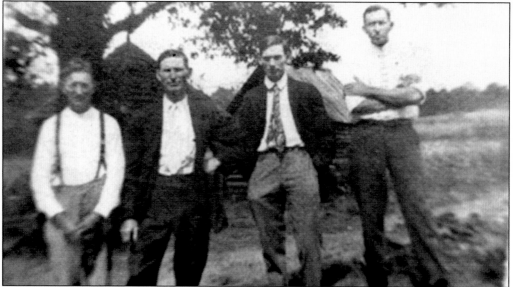

Around 1920 the Baker boys, grandsons of Ezra and Rebecca, stand in the yard. They are, from left to right, Jim, George Stephen, John, and Hiram. The George Stephen Baker homeplace was located where its namesake Baker Elementary School now stands. Their parents were John Dixon and Lucy Ann Hilderbrand Baker. (Lil Prather collection.)

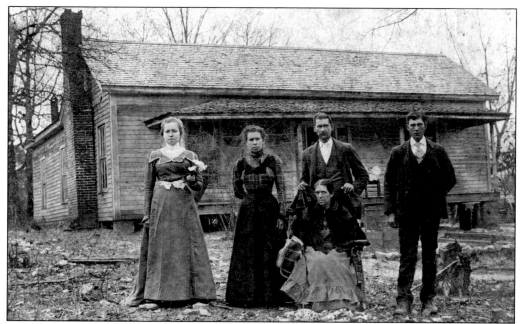

Robert Milton Scroggs (1844–1922) married Rachel Smith (1847–1901) in 1868. The Scroggs family lived near the old Cowen (original spelling) church, school, and cemetery at the intersection of Baker and Cowan Roads. Their homestead was the old Brand place. They are photographed with their children around 1900. From left to right are Margaret Scroggs Prather, Lula Scroggs Canup, and Oscar Charles Scroggs. (Reginald Awtrey collection.)

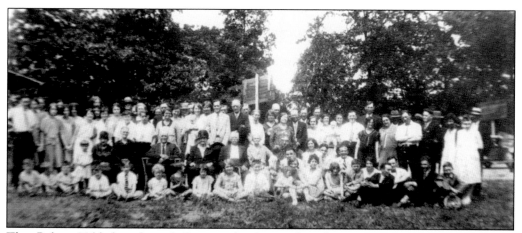

The Baker, Hilderbrand, and Scroggs families gather for a reunion in 1929–1930. (Lil Prather collection.)

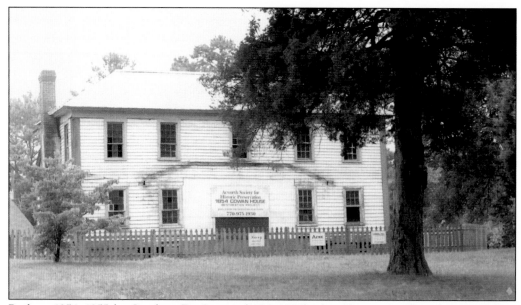

Built *c.* 1854–1855 by Stephen D. Cowen (1824–1900), this Plantation Plain home exhibits period construction techniques, floor plan, and styling details. Cowen was one of approximately 250 Acworth area men who served with Confederate forces, but unlike others, his farm was intact after the war. He later accumulated a total of 479 acres of orchards, woodlands, and fields. Cowen reared 14 children here and outlived two of his three wives. (ASHP collection.)

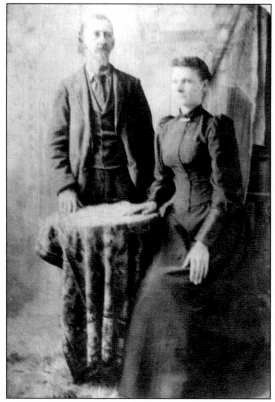

John Brown (1841–1924) moved from Henry County before the Civil War. He farmed cotton and corn on 100 acres north of Acworth. During the Civil War, he served in Company A of the 18th Georgia Regiment and lost an eye in battle. He is pictured here with his second wife, Minnie A. Thompson (1869–1940), whom he married in 1892. He had four children with his first wife and seven children with Minnie. (Hinton Brown collection.)

Samuel C. Moon (1823–1894) married Mary T. Chastain (1827–1888) in Cobb County in 1843. Moon owned 320 acres of oak and hickory land. The Moons are pictured here. Books were still a rarity and the Moons posed with *The Dictionary* and *Wonders of the World*. Their daughter, Maggie Bell Moon, (1847–1928) married Thompson M. Morris (1851–1879), a marriage that lasted less than two years, after he was gunned down in a shootout. (Thompson Arrendale collection.)

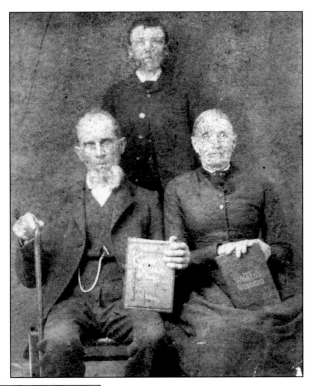

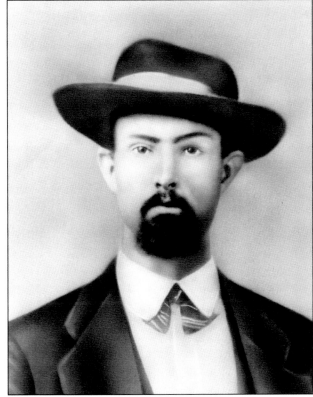

Acworth's town marshal Thompson Morris (pictured here), his two brothers, and a Sunday school party traveled by train to Kingston, Georgia for a picnic. Morris fired his pistol in the streets and was fined by Kingston marshal John Burrough. An argument ensued and gunfire was exchanged. Burrough fatally shot Thompson and Joseph Morris. The accounts differed as to who fired first, but 47 Acworthians objected in a letter to the editor to *The Atlanta Constitution's* account and its characterization of the Morris boys as "Acworth Roughs." (Thompson Arrendale collection.)

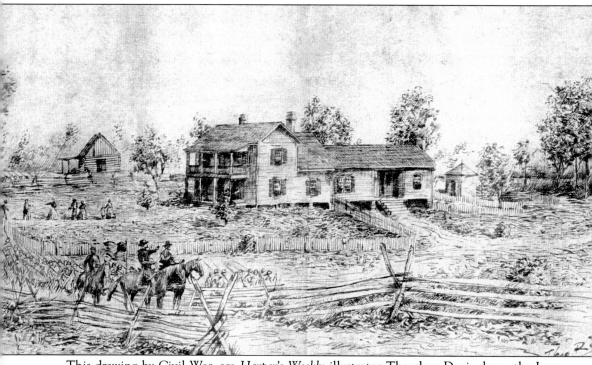

This drawing by Civil War–era *Harper's Weekly* illustrator Theodore Davis shows the Lemon House near downtown Acworth on June 6, 1864. Sherman's staff officers had commandeered the Lemon House for staff headquarters from June 6 to June 9. Sherman stayed nearby, but he ate meals with his staff in the Lemon dining room. The federal provost marshal's office was located in the front parlor. Capt. James Lile Lemon's wife Eliza, seven months pregnant and with a small daughter to care for, bravely remained in her home to protect it. The house was spared when Acworth was burned. (Mark Lemon collection.)

Two

WAR BETWEEN THE STATES

As the Civil War began, Acworth citizens responded enthusiastically to Georgia's call for volunteers. Acworth's two pre-war militia companies, the "Acworth Infantry" and the "Acworth Invincibles," were augmented with fresh recruits and sent to Camp McDonald at Big Shanty (Kennesaw) for training. They then boarded trains to Richmond, Virginia to join the Army of Northern Virginia. The Infantry became Company A, 18th Georgia Volunteer Infantry, and the Invincibles became Company C, 41st Georgia Volunteer Infantry. Both regiments had superb combat records, with the 18th perhaps the most illustrious. It fought first with Gen. John Bell Hood's famous Texas Brigade and then under Gen. William T. Wofford's reorganized Georgia Brigade playing a decisive role in many Confederate victories. In battle Acworth soldiers from both regiments displayed great courage and fighting spirit. Later, as the fortunes of war turned against them, they sacrificed and endured terrible want and privations, fighting on desperately until the final surrender at Appomattox.

Acworth remained relatively insulated from strife for three years except for the excitement of the theft of the locomotive "The General" in Big Shanty by Union spy James J. Andrews and his men in April 1862. Andrews's raiders were headed to Union lines near Chattanooga and tore up track and cut telegraph lines along the way. A party led by the train conductor, William Fuller, followed the raiders on a hand-powered rail car. Reaching Acworth, Fuller was given guns gathered from citizens. Two Acworthians, Steve Stokely and Campbell Smith, joined the pursuit. The stolen locomotive and the raiders were captured later that day and some of them, including Andrews, were hanged.

By 1864 Acworth's relative safety behind the front lines was breached. Strategically located astride the railroad connecting Chattanooga and Atlanta, Acworth lay directly in Union Gen. William T. Sherman's path as he moved southward to capture Atlanta. After battles in nearby Dallas at the end of May 1864, the Union army marched to Acworth on June 6 to await the repair of the recently burned Etowah River bridge and the reestablishment of supply trains from Chattanooga. Pouring into town, Federal troops commandeered whatever house or building suited their purpose. Confederate Capt. James Lile Lemon's house was occupied for headquarters. Eliza Lemon was ordered to sleep in her kitchen and cook for General Sherman's staff as her house and grounds were systematically stripped and looted. Many other Acworth families were likewise beleaguered. Acworth was under martial law and citizens were prohibited from entering the town and business district without a pass signed by the Union provost marshal.

The occupation of Acworth wore on for six months while the bulk of the Union Army fought at Kennesaw Mountain and captured Atlanta. Conditions for Acworth citizens during this period were brutal to the extreme. Northern soldiers took whatever food Acworthians had without recompense. Food scraps had to be hoarded and hidden. Because of the influx of thousands of soldiers, sanitary conditions during the occupancy were horrible. Sickness, starvation, and disease reportedly increased daily.

Acworth witnessed its closest combat after the fall of Atlanta to Union forces. Confederate Gen. John Bell Hood put his army on the move to attack Sherman's supply line and storehouses at Allatoona Pass, a few miles directly north of Acworth. After capturing Big Shanty and Acworth rail stations and destroying railroad track, the Confederates reached Allatoona and found it guarded by a full division of Union troops that Sherman had ordered from Rome once he guessed Hood's intentions. Over 5,000 men fought here on October 5 with 1,500 casualties. The battle ended with a Confederate retreat.

In that autumn of 1864 Sherman prepared to move his army southward on his infamous "March to the Sea." As Atlanta was burned, so too were Marietta, Big Shanty, and Acworth. Acworth's destruction on November 13 would have no doubt been complete had it not been for Union Maj. James Connolly who tried to prevent some of the burning. No more than 12 private homes were saved in town. Even the churches were not immune from destruction. The Methodist church was the only one spared because it had a Masonic Lodge in its upper story. After the army left, the town was a burned-out, smoldering shell. Its citizens were absolutely destitute.

With the subsequent end of the war and the return of Confederate veterans to their devastated homes, the staggering task of rebuilding awaited Acworthians. With virtually no food, clothing, or shelter, they grimly but resolutely set about the task of rebuilding their lives. Smith Lemon, always the prescient businessman, returned from Confederate service and unearthed $5,000 in gold coins he had buried at the war's onset as a hedge against possible disaster. With this fortune, Smith and the recently returned James Lile reestablished the bank and mercantile store and opened a brickyard. Credit was extended to neighbors under the most liberal terms. The town was slowly rebuilt, eventually meeting and then surpassing its former economic status and vitality.[9]

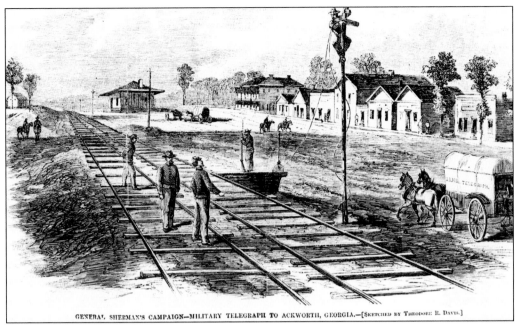

GENERAL SHERMAN'S CAMPAIGN—MILITARY TELEGRAPH TO ACKWORTH, GEORGIA.—[Sketched by Theodore R. Davis.]

This drawing, attributed to *Harper's Weekly* illustrator Theodore Davis, depicts Federals working on the telegraph lines in Acworth during the occupation. Telegraph lines were begun through Acworth in 1851. The telegraph, the line of communication, and the railroad tracks, the line of supply, were destroyed and repaired as the town's fortunes turned with the tides of war. (Joe McTyre collection.)

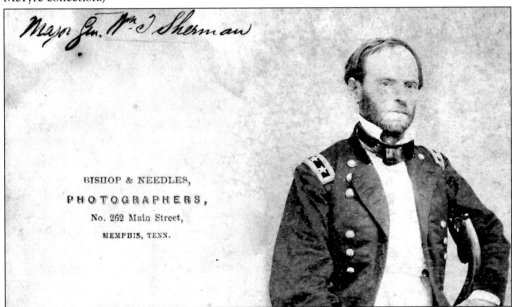

This carte-de-visite of William Tecumseh Sherman with the photographers' name and address on the back was made in Memphis before the Atlanta Campaign. Cartes-de-visite or visiting cards were small portraits (two and one-half by four inches) that were popular in this era. A number of photographs (usually eight) were taken on one glass negative. They were cheap, mass-produced, and easy to collect, especially if made of an important person. (Mark Lemon collection.)

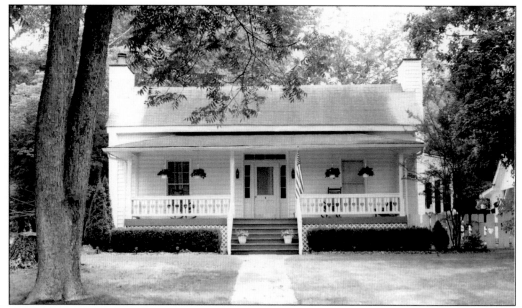

General Sherman reportedly occupied this home on Dallas Street from June 6 to June 9. The house was originally two tenant homes on the Lemon estate that were joined together with the two front rooms in one home linked to the two back rooms of the other home via a pantry. As shown in this modern photograph, additions have increased the size of the home. Later homeowner Ruth D. McClure served as Acworth postmaster for a number of years starting in 1933. (ASHP collection.)

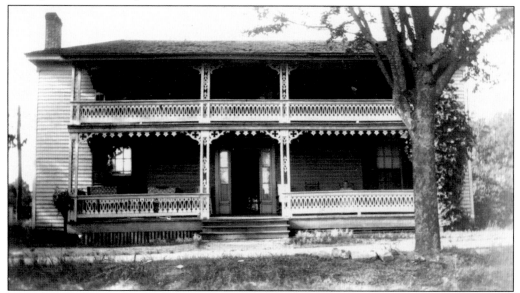

The McEver House at 4989 North Main Street was used as a field hospital by Union troops and was spared destruction. This 1925 photograph shows how the house would have looked in 1864 with its two-story veranda. Built in the 1840s, the home style is a type of I-house known as Plantation Plain. An I-house is two stories high, two rooms wide, and one room deep. Plantation Plain is further elaborated with stylistic detailing and varying porches, chimneys, and rearward extensions. (William and Helen Roberson collection.)

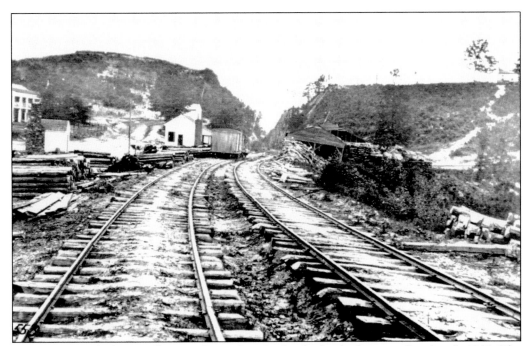

This photograph shows Allatoona Pass after the battle fought here on October 5, 1864. The Clayton house on the left was built in 1832 and still stands. Also visible is an earthen fort on the top left ridge and artillery stables on the top right ridge. The battle site is well preserved with entrenchments still visible today. (Pat Casey Tumlin collection.)

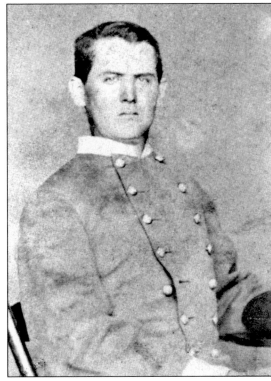

This photograph of Capt. James Lile Lemon, C.S.A, was taken in early 1864 when he was a prisoner of war incarcerated at Fort Delaware Military Prison. He had been wounded and captured during the assault on Fort Sanders in Knoxville, Tennessee. After the war, he walked the nearly 800 miles home despite being exhausted, deaf in one ear, and nearly blind. For his brave part in the assault on Fort Sanders, he was posthumously awarded the C.S.A. Medal of Honor. (Mark Lemon collection.)

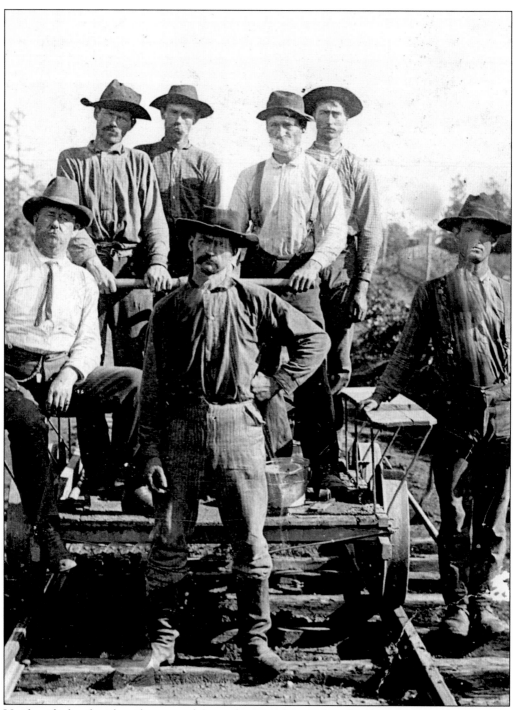

Unidentified railroad workers posed for a photograph on a hand-powered rail car in the early 1900s. The route of the W&A Railroad followed the old Cherokee trading route, the Peachtree Trail. The first rail line, the Western and Atlantic, ran from Atlanta to Chattanooga and was completed by the early 1850s. In 1870 the line became the Nashville, Chattanooga and St. Louis system. Today CSX manages over 60 daily freight trains. (Mark Lemon collection.)

Three

AT WORK

Acworth's original platted commercial district was on the north side of the railroad tracks at Northside/ Southside Drives and Cherokee Street. The small commercial district was known as Awtrey Corner for one of Acworth's first merchants, Merrill C. Awtrey. He established a general merchandise store in 1848 and ran it with various partners over the years. Businesses on Main Street soon followed. Wooden structures, burned in fires or destroyed by Union troops during the Civil War, were replaced with brick structures in the later part of the 19th century.

By 1882, with Acworth's war recovery well underway, business interests included J.Q. Tanner Dry Goods; Awtrey, Cooper & Co. General Merchandise and cotton buyers; Dr. J.H. Humphries; W.J. Tanner, Blacksmith and Wagon Maker; T.H. Gibson, Blacksmith and Woodworker; the S. Lemon Banking Company; and J.H. Bate and Co. Watchmakers and Jewelers.[10] During this period of economic growth, traveling salesmen known as drummers and other visitors arrived by train and stayed in the Litchfield House hotel.

In 1915, with the advent of the automobile era, an unpaved Main Street became part of the Dixie Highway, the first interstate highway to link the urban North to the rural South and Florida vacation spots. The federal government designated the Dixie as U.S. 41 through north Georgia in the 1920s. In the late 1940s, the new Highway 41 bypassed downtown Acworth and the two-lane Dixie Highway became "Old Highway 41." Tourist-dependent businesses moved out to the new "Four Lane." Although interstate travelers would no longer traverse the downtown and contribute to Acworth's economy, Main Street remained important to the regional economy throughout the 1950s.

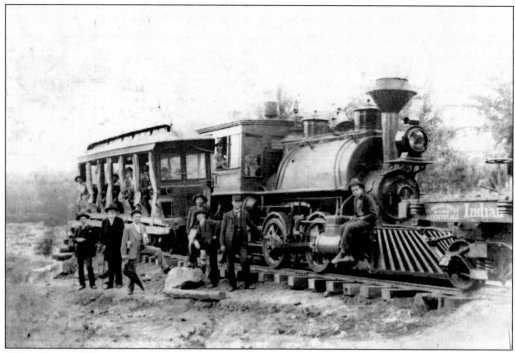

This photograph of an early railroad engine with an open-air passenger car was reportedly taken in the Acworth area in the late 1800s. Passenger service for Acworth started before the Civil War and waned with the advent of the automobile. (Vanishing Georgia collection, Georgia Dept. of Archives and History.)

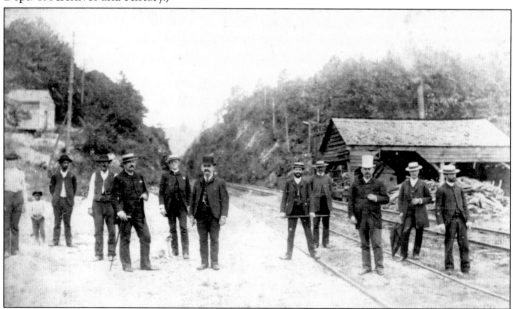

An early photograph shows rail workers at Allatoona Pass. The 180-foot deep railroad cut was blasted through the rugged Allatoona Mountains. Over time, the rail bed through Acworth has been built up to lessen the grade at the pass. (Vanishing Georgia collection, Georgia Dept. of Archives and History.)

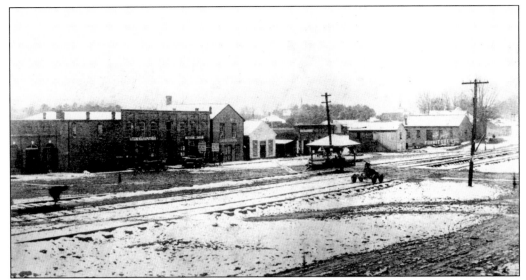

Snow covered Main Street and the Cherokee Street railroad crossing (one block from the current Lemon Street crossing) in a rare photograph from the 1890s. The prominent two-story brick Armstrong Building is shown before its 1906 facelift. It hosts the Litchfield and Putnam general store and Robert Butler business. Downtown buildings are a mixture of brick and wood. (Vanishing Georgia collection, Georgia Dept. of Archives and History.)

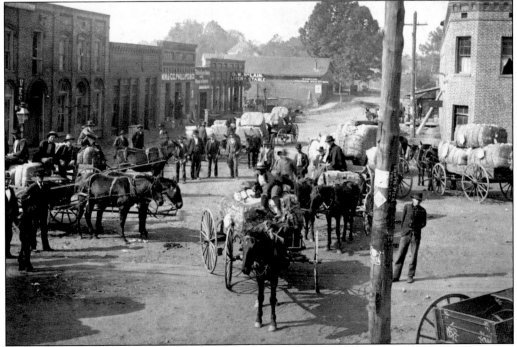

Farmers brought their cotton crops to Main Street in this early 1900s photo taken from the Cherokee Street rail crossing. Again the Armstrong Building is prominent in the upper left before its 1906 renovation. Now the buildings are mostly brick, including the warehouse buildings lining the railroad side of Main Street. Note the G.W. McLain Livery Stable at the end of the Armstrong Building block. (Imogene Eaton collection.)

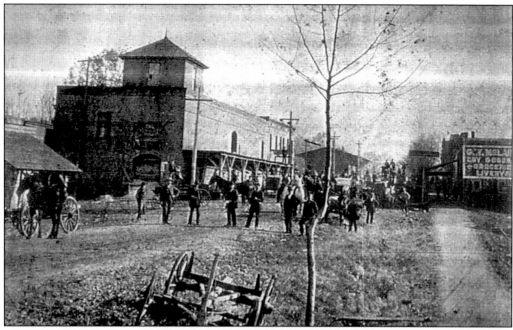

This view of Main Street from the early 1900s looks toward the center of town, with the G.W. McLain Livery Stable on the right and warehouses on the left. With horses and carriages for hire, McLain served locals and train passengers with transport to the countryside. (Acworth HPC collection.)

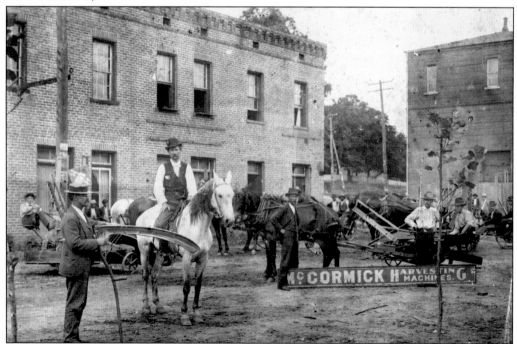

This scene from the vantage point of the railroad tracks shows the rear of the warehouse buildings on Main Street. The men appear to be advertising McCormick's harvesting machines and farm equipment. (Imogene Eaton collection.)

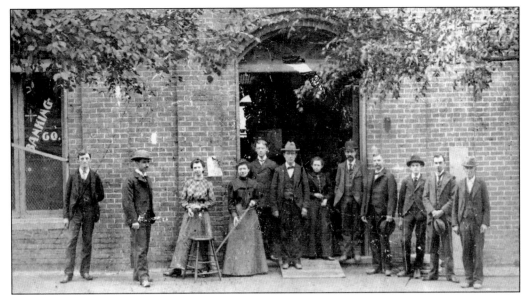

Jim and Bob McMillan founded the McMillan Brothers general merchandise store in 1896. The business shared a building with the S. Lemon Banking Company (now 4817 and 4819 South Main Street). Pictured from left to right outside the building in 1906 are Walter Nichols, Bob McMillan, Mrs. H.B. Terry, unidentified, Claude McMillan, Jim McMillan, Maggie Watson, Walter Abbott, Jesse L. Lemon, Fred Hull, P.C. Carnes, and Ivy Goodwin. (Nancy McMillan MacPherson collection)

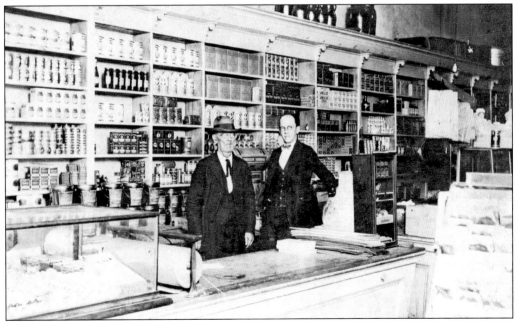

Pictured in 1928 inside the McMillan Brothers store are Jim and his son George Huie. A forerunner of the modern department store, McMillan Brothers sold groceries, hardware, farming tools, dry goods, school books, ready-to-wear apparel, shoes, and furniture into the 1930s. George Huie would later hold office as Cobb County Sheriff and Commissioner. (Nancy McMillan MacPherson collection.)

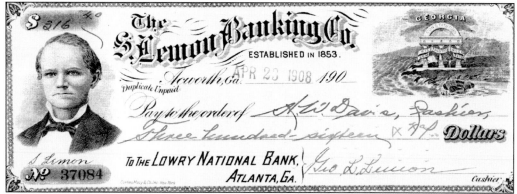

A 1908 check was drawn from the S. Lemon Banking Company. Smith Lemon established the company in 1853, making it the oldest bank in Cobb County. It was a private bank until 1906 when a state charter was granted. The charter was later transferred to the Cobb Exchange Bank. (Mark Lemon collection.)

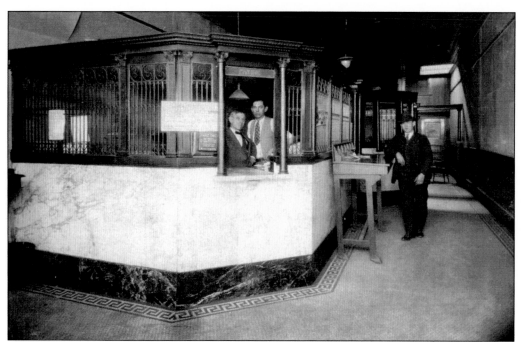

Fred Hull, an unidentified man, and Lemon Awtrey Sr. stand in the interior of the S. Lemon Banking Company. Before the Civil War, Smith Lemon had the foresight to bury $5,000 in gold coins. Upon his return from military service, he dug up the coins and used them to reopen the bank and his mercantile store. The Lemons then extended generous credit to their fellow citizens and fueled Acworth's recovery. (Acworth HPC collection.)

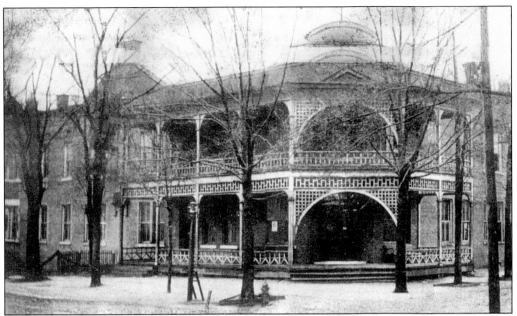

The Litchfield House/Acworth Inn, a two-story, L-shaped brick hotel with chamfered entryway, wide verandas on both stories and roof-top cupola cut an elegant presence at the corner of Main and Lemon Streets. The chamfered corner treatment was echoed in buildings throughout downtown. E.L. Litchfield (1817–1883), his wife Elizabeth Smith Litchfield (1824–1900), and later his son Lemeul (1848–1891) and wife Kansas Roberts owned and operated the hotel. (Acworth HPC collection.)

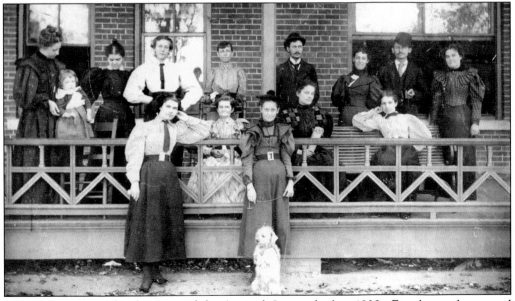

W.P. McDowell and family managed the Acworth Inn in the late 1800s. Family members posed on the veranda. Willie McDowell, seated on the right, married Dr. E.M. Bailey ("Dr. Gene"). Fannie McDowell, in the white blouse standing in front of the railing, became the wife of James E. Carnes, a longtime Bank of Acworth employee and one of the first captains of the Acworth Volunteer Fire Fighters.[11](Acworth HPC collection.)

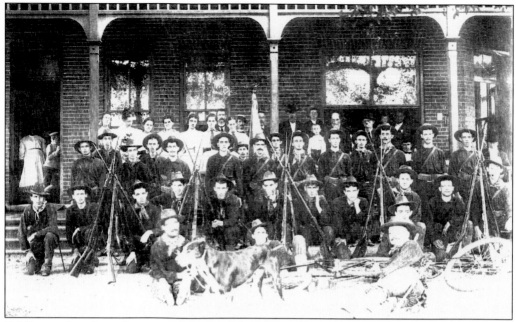

Soldiers gathered on the steps of the Litchfield House/Acworth Inn in 1898. They were most likely a militia troop for the Spanish-American War. The hotel was the scene of many group portraits, gatherings, and celebrations for almost a century until the City of Acworth condemned the dilapidated structure in 1961. (Acworth HPC collection.)

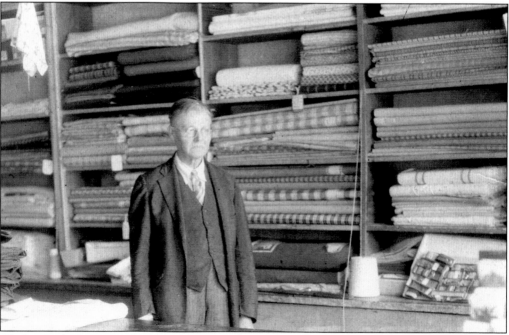

Clark's Cash Store was located at the corner of Main and Dallas Streets (across from the Armstrong Building) from the 1890s to the early 1940s. Andrew Jack "A.J." Clark is photographed in the store in 1930. Clark came from Paulding County and soon was an active member of the Acworth Methodist Church. (Robert M. Clark collection.)

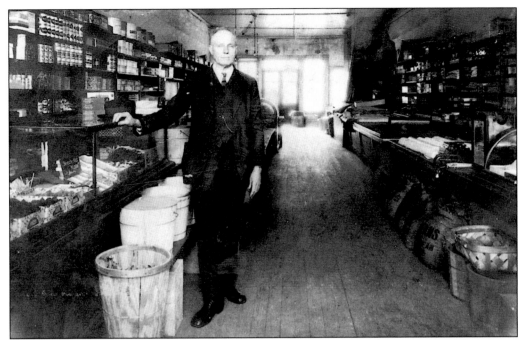

James Crittendon Stokely was a photographer, grocery and dry goods storeowner, and real estate salesman. He owned the building at present-day 4805 South Main Street from the late 1890s to the 1930s. This photograph shows the store's interior in the 1930s. The rear doors and windows are the same today. Collins Furniture occupied the building in the 1940s. (Dr. Dylan Reach collection.)

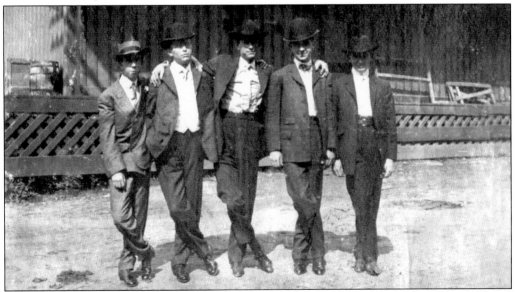

Fred G. Hull had a varied career in Acworth. He is photographed here on the right with friends in front of the depot around the turn of the 19th century. "Mr. Acworth" delivered general merchandise for the McMillan Brothers, owned a jewelry store, repaired clocks and watches, was an optometrist, and served as Acworth City Clerk from 1917 to 1962. He married the former Bessie Carnes in 1907. (Reginald Awtrey collection.)

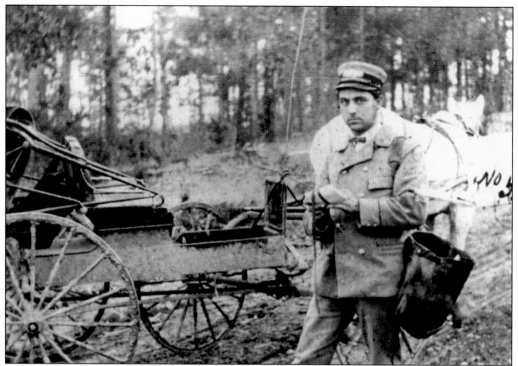

Rural mail carrier Joseph B. Rainey delivers the mail to J.P. Dewberry's box in this 1906 photo. Dewberry owned a large farm north of downtown. Later the property was home to Acworth's drive-in movie theater and a subdivision starting in the 1950s. (Vanishing Georgia collection, Georgia Dept. of Archives and History.)

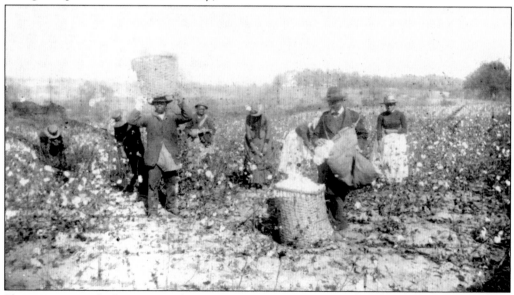

Sharecroppers picked cotton on the R.H. Northcutt farm in Northwest Cobb County, c. 1890. Cotton farming peaked during this period until the 1920s. Bad weather, boll weevils, and Depression-era prices effectively killed cotton cultivation in Cobb County. (Vanishing Georgia collection, Georgia Dept. of Archives and History.)

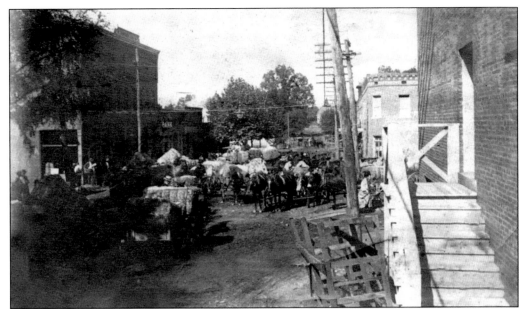

An early 20th-century view illustrates "Cotton Days" on North Main Street. Note the 1906 changes to the Armstrong Building facade. A carpenter and banker, John Armstrong built several large homes along Main Street, only one of which survives at Church Street. He also enlarged the building at Main and Dallas Streets that bears a metal nameplate on the cornice stamped "Armstrong Building 1906." (Reginald Awtrey Collection.)

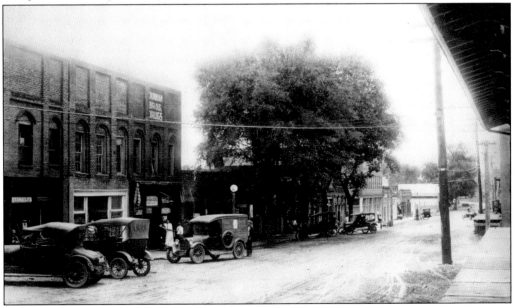

This photograph taken from the train depot (eaves at upper right) shows Main Street in the late 1920s. Albert J. Durham established Durham Drugs in the third building from the left in 1895; his brother Claude G. joined him in the business two years later. Believed to be the oldest drugstore in Cobb County, Durham Brothers became a Rexall Store in 1914. By the 1920s, its modern soda fountain ensured its status as a teen hangout. George Gober Lacey purchased the business in 1943; Lacey Drugs still exists today. (Acworth HPC collection.)

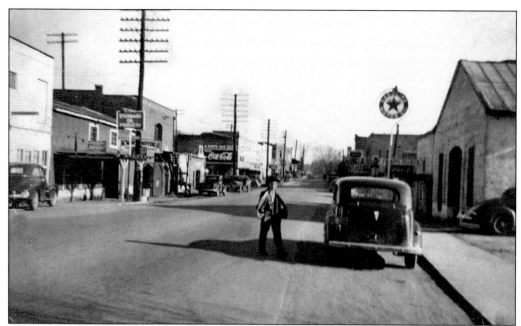

This *c.* 1930 view of the north end of Main Street looks back toward the center of town. On the left side of the photograph, signs for Standard Oil products and the Acworth Café are visible. The buildings in the right foreground housed the Acworth Motor Company owned by Carl Butler. (Willie B. Kemp collection.)

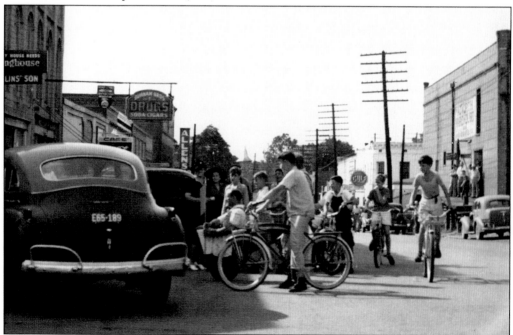

Melvin Haynes's wheelbarrow ride was his spoils for a winning bet with Cliff Smith on the outcome of the 1942 Georgia governor's race in this photo taken Wednesday, November 4. Haynes, the owner of a funeral home on Due West Road, was mayor of Acworth in 1947; Smith, the wheelbarrow pusher, lived on the end of Academy Street. (Robert J. Kienel collection.)

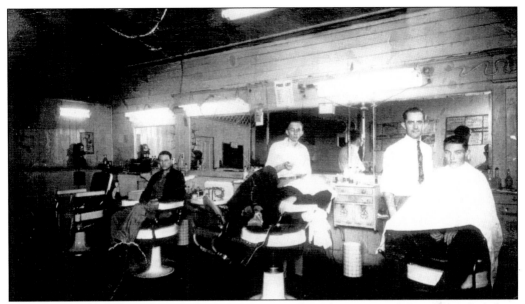

Chandler's Barber Shop was located near Durham Brothers drug store on Main Street. J. Aubrey Chandler, the proprietor, was mayor of Acworth from 1957 to 1960. Pictured inside in 1946 are, from left to right, Claude Greenway, Frank Nations (getting a shave), Oscar Hunt, Harold Prescott, and Clyde Chandler. (Robert M. Clark collection.)

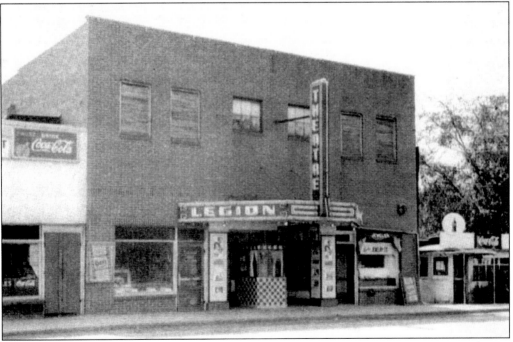

V.S. "Buster" Golden built the Legion Theatre in the 1930s. In addition to movies, the theatre was used for community events. Before desegregation, black customers were required to sit in the balcony, accessed by a door and staircase in the building to the left of the theatre. The Silver Trolley, a popular diner and teen hangout, is to the right of the theatre. (Hudson family collection.)

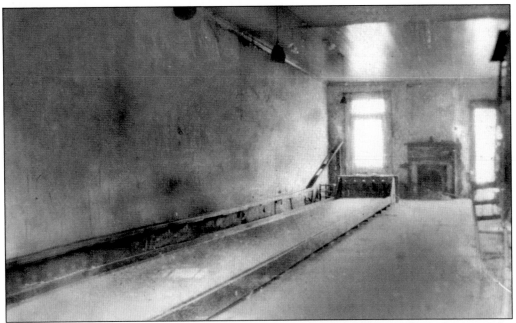

The bowling alley was located in the Lemon cotton warehouse building in the early part of the 20th century. The depot, warehouses, and other buildings lining the railroad side of Main Street were removed in the early 1980s to make way for parking lots. (Reginald Awtrey collection.)

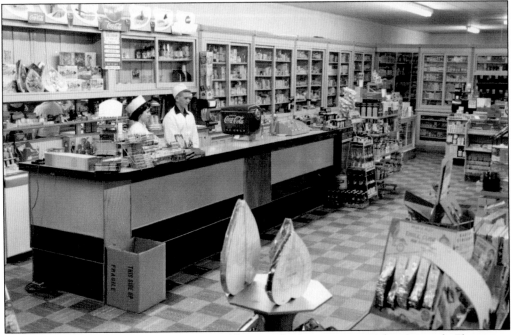

Soda jerks Barbara Brand and Bobby Robbins work the counter at the Acworth Pharmacy, the "Cheerful Druggist," c. 1950. Pharmacist L.S. James moved into the curved glass storefront at current 4841 North Main Street in 1939. The pharmacy had two later homes: on Main Street north of Mill Street and in a newly built structure at 4427 Carnes Street. (Willie B. Kemp collection.)

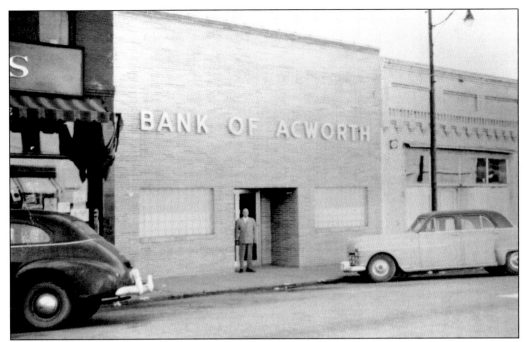

The Bank of Acworth was founded in 1905 to serve farmers, merchants, and industries. In this photo, it is housed in a "modern" facade next to the Armstrong Building. (Dene Sheheane collection.)

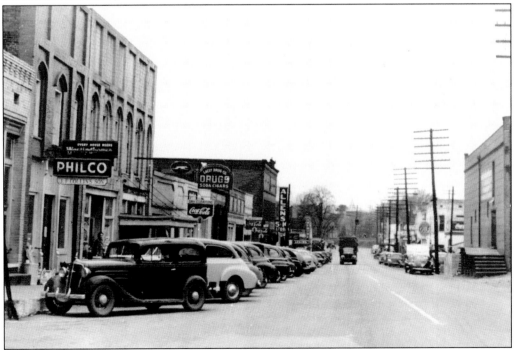

Main Street in the late 1940s was awash with perpendicular hanging storefront signs to lure the Dixie Highway automobile travelers inside. Allens Five and Ten store occupied the Armstrong Building. (Shirley Fowler Walker collection.)

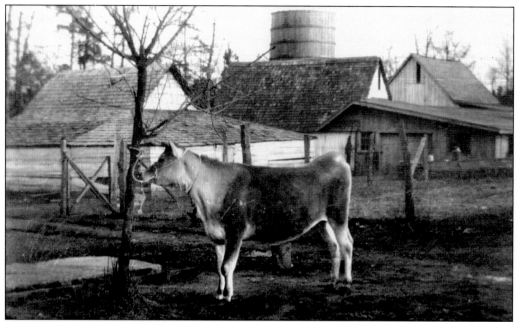

Roy Tippin bred registered Jersey cattle on Rock Dale Farm, located opposite the South Main Street and 2002 Cowan Road intersection. Days Chevrolet later occupied the site. Tippen had 35 head of cattle and a bull. This 1919 photo shows one of his prized pure-bred cattle on the farm with the toolshed, barn, creamery, and the silo for winter corn feed. (Willie B. Kemp collection.)

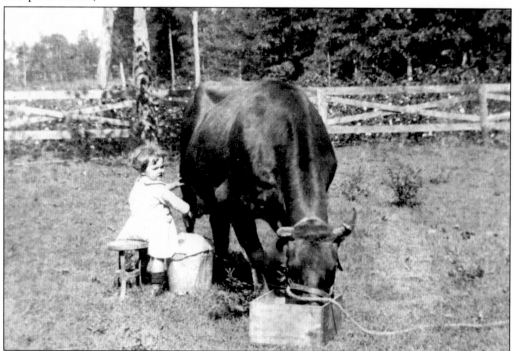

Ida Louise milks one of her daddy's cows in April 1919. Ida was the daughter of Roy and Mamie Tippin. (Willie B. Kemp collection.)

A 1921 combination sale bulletin for the Rock Dale Farm and Brookhill Farm touts "high class, prize winning and register of merit" cows for purchase in Acworth. (Willie B. Kemp collection.)

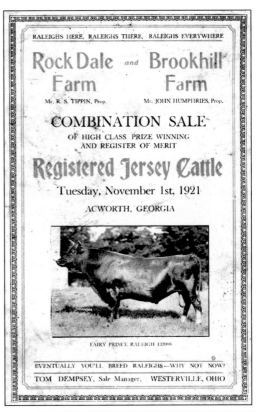

This view shows one of Acworth's planing mills that may have been on present-day Southside Drive. The Southern Cotton Oil Company occupied the site for a time in the 1920s, converting cotton seeds into hull, meal, and oil, but the site became Mills Lumber Company by 1930. There was also a planing mill on the railroad side of Main Street across from Mill Street. (Vanishing Georgia collection, Georgia Dept. of Archives and History.)

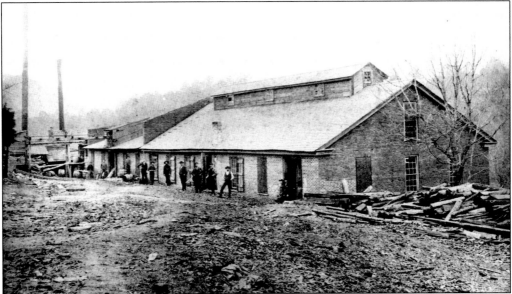

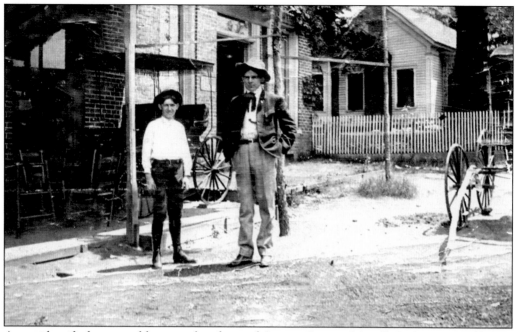

An unidentified man and boy stand in front of Awtrey Corner. Merrill C. Awtrey established the Awtrey mercantile business in 1848 in a wooden structure in the original platted commercial district on Southside Drive. The brick structure was built before the turn of the 19th century. The house has since been removed for a medical center's parking lot. (Reginald Awtrey Collection.)

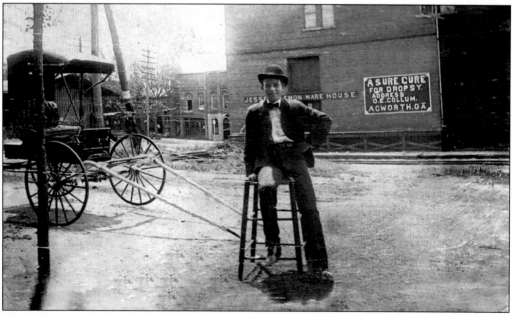

This photograph of Ernest Collins was shot from the vantage point of the Awtrey Store on Southside Drive towards the railroad tracks and the back of the Jesse C. Lemon cotton warehouse on Main Street. The building advertisement reads "A sure cure for dropsy. Address D.E. Collum. Acworth, GA." (Reginald Awtrey Collection.)

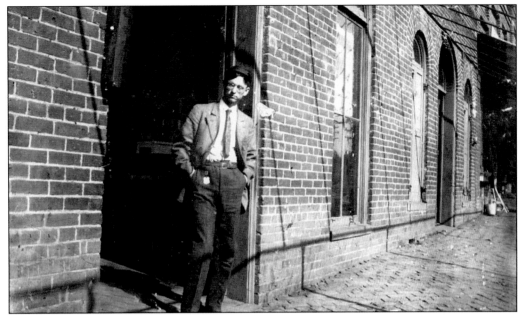

Orlando Awtrey Jr., born in 1888 and known as "Gan," stands in front of Orlando Awtrey and Son on Southside Drive. The Awtrey store occupied the site from 1848 until the 1960s. Over time, the five buildings here also housed a furniture store, an undertaking parlor, a buggy factory, a hardware store, and a chapel. (Reginald Awtrey Collection.)

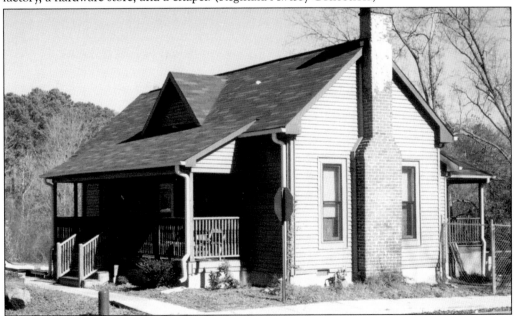

By the early 1920s, African-American businesses were located in the area of Bethel A.M.E. Church. Early businessmen included John F. Buffington, an ice cream parlor owner; Henry Williams, who had a hardware store; and Jeff McConnell, who owned and operated a cobbler shop and cafe. McConnell owned this house at the corner of Cherokee and Taylor Streets. The home was recently renovated using Community Development Block Grant funding. (ASHP collection.)

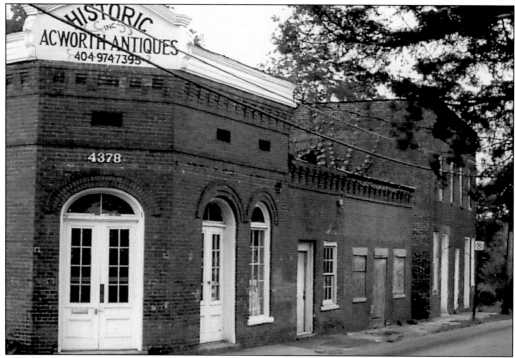

In 1885 a wooden structure on this site across Cherokee Street from Awtrey Corner housed the H.W. Kitchen and H.M. Williams general merchandise store. In the 1930s Acworth Laundry was located in the brick building later built on the site, and Conway-Noland Toys moved here in the 1940s. The right two-story building was the longtime home of a feed and grain store with the Colored Masons and Oddfellows upstairs. (Emory and Beverly Noland collection.)

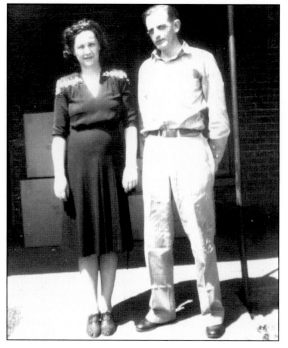

In 1935 Margaret Conway made stuffed toys for her children using scraps from her chenille bedspread business. Later, she sold them with the homemade bedspreads to Dixie Highway travelers. By the early 1940s, she had acquired a partner, Fay Noland (with whom she is photographed here) moved to Acworth from Adairsville, and hired 87 employees. In 1944 Conway-Noland Toys turned out 8,400 stuffed chenille toys a week. (Emory and Beverly Noland collection.)

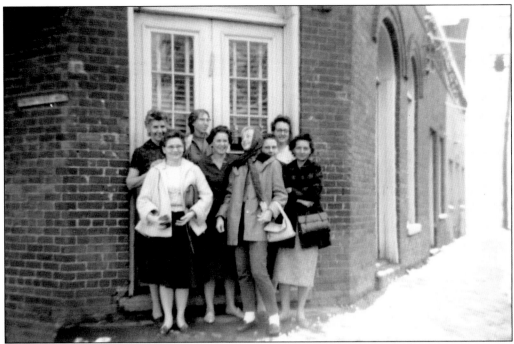

In this building on Cherokee Street, Conway-Noland Toys (later Lovable Toys) made original designs including dolls, elephants, bunny rabbits, hounds, Scottie dogs, soldiers, sailors, WACs, and WAVEs. Pictured here in the early 1960s are Lovable Toys employees. In the 1960s the company became Boyce Manufacturing and added life jackets to its product line. Boyce moved to the Unique Knitting Mill after Unique's demise and was sold in the late 1980s. (Emory and Beverly Noland collection.)

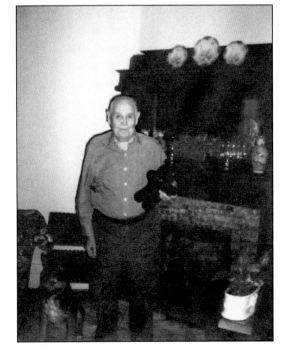

Emory Noland stands in front of his mantel in 2002 with "Emory Bear." His brother Fay gave him the stuffed chenille animal when he enlisted in the Army Air Force in 1940. The Conway-Noland bear traveled with Emory during his tour of duty in Europe in World War II. (ASHP collection.)

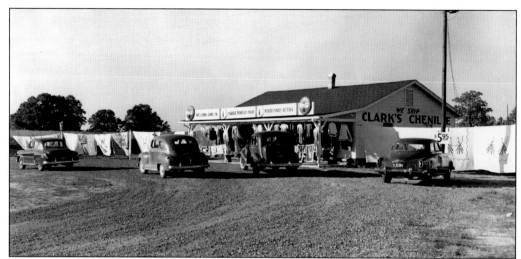

Clark's Chenille was originally located on the Dixie Highway south of New McEver Road but is shown here after its move to the new U.S. 41 in the early 1950s. Catherine Evans Whitener of Dalton created the first tufted bedspread and taught other women her technique. Chenille bedspreads, robes, bathmats, and rugs were sold by the side of the road to Dixie Highway travelers. (Robert M. Clark collection.)

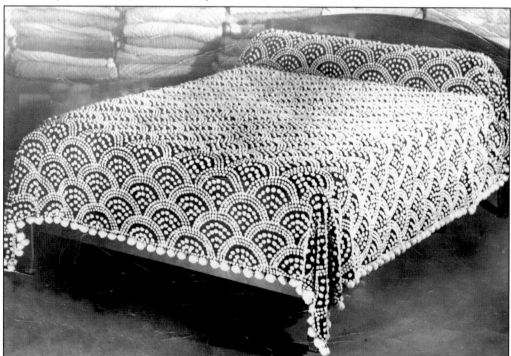

"Spreadlines" flourished as far south as Acworth, but were most numerous from Dalton to Cartersville where the Dixie route was known as "Peacock Alley" after the most popular bedspread design. Dixie travelers knew how to "follow the bedspreads to Atlanta." Chenille bedspreads were originally handmade, like the one here for sale at Clark's, but mechanization soon followed. The tufting technique evolved into the modern carpet industry in Dalton. (Robert M. Clark collection.)

Grogan's Tourist Cottages, the first of their kind in the county, served travelers on the Dixie Highway with one-room cabins. After the closure of the tourist court at South Main and Grogan Streets, one of the cottages was relocated to an empty lot between 4873 and 4887 North Main Street. The cottage became Sam's Barbershop (now demolished). Fred Kienel took this photograph of the move. (Robert J. Kienel collection.)

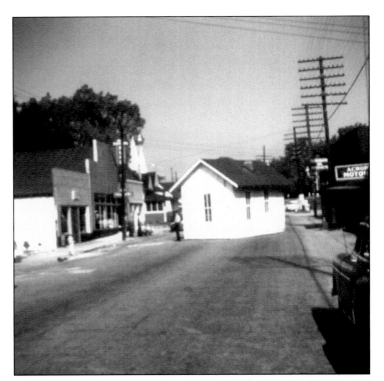

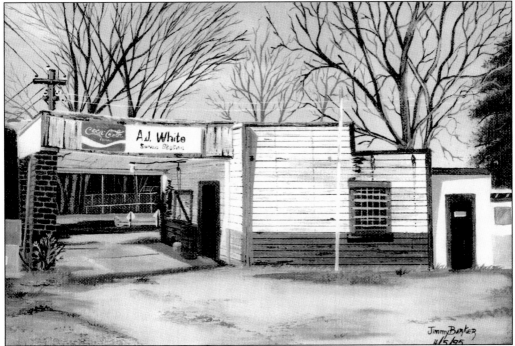

This early drive-in gas station at 4288 South Main Street was originally Grogan's Service Station, across Main Street from the tourist cottages. By the mid-1930s the gas station had evolved beyond this example into the full service station with repair bays, offices, restrooms, and floor space for selling tires, motor oil, and other accessories. (Original artwork by Jimmy Barker.)

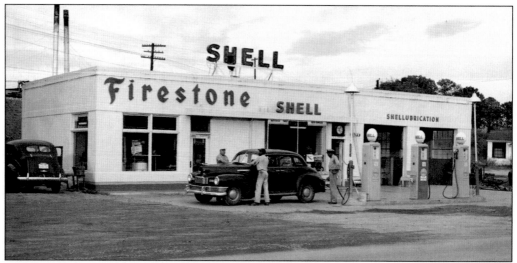

The Shell Station at Main Street and Albany Drive was built as a wooden structure in 1938; the stucco building here is photographed shortly after its construction in 1942. The Fowler family ran it as a full-service gas station and restaurant until the late 1960s. Providing the gas pumping and window washing here are, from left to right, owner Ed Fowler, Claude Hardin, and Harold Davis. (Shirley Fowler Walker collection.)

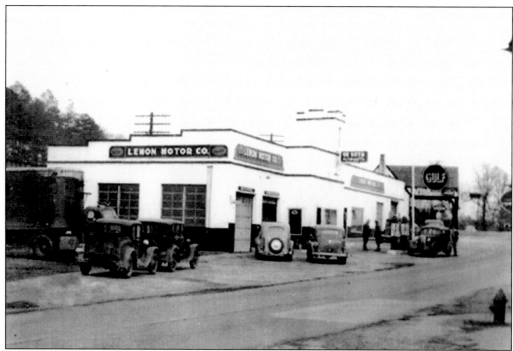

Lemon Motor Company was located at the corner of Main and Smith Streets in the 1940s, across Main Street from the Greyhound Bus Station and across Smith Street from the Pure Oil Gas Station. The Pure Oil chain erected distinctive stations with an eye-catching white English-cottage motif, blue trim, and blue porcelain enamel-tile roofs. (ASHP collection.)

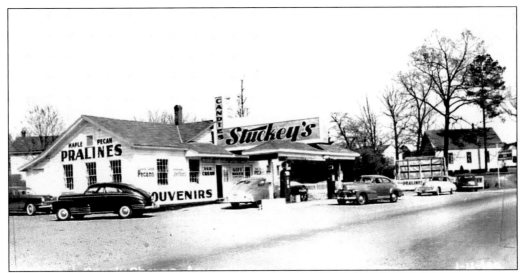

Pecan log rolls, pralines, fudge, and divinity awaited Dixie Highway travelers at Stuckey's after the war in the mid-1940s. This postcard depicts one of the early original locations for the Georgia chain on Main Street (at the 2002 Cowan Road intersection). The mill village church is on the right. With the construction of the new U.S. 41 in the late 1940s, Stuckey's moved out to the "Four Lane." (Acworth HPC collection.)

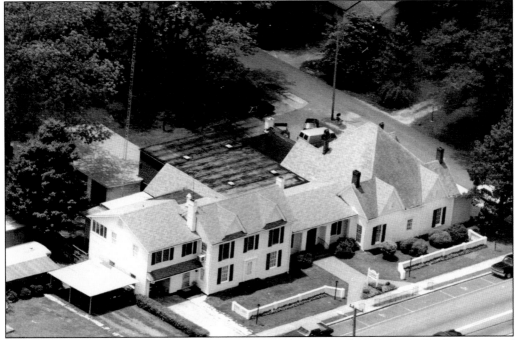

With its start in 1886 as a furniture store, the Collins Funeral Home has the distinction of being the oldest continuous business in Acworth. Two residential buildings, built in the city's prosperous 1880s, were joined in the 1920s to house the funeral home; the furniture store remained in the business district. Prior to J.F. Collins's expansion into funerals, caskets were made special order by chair and cabinet makers. The funeral home remained in the family for over a century. (McCoy family collection.)

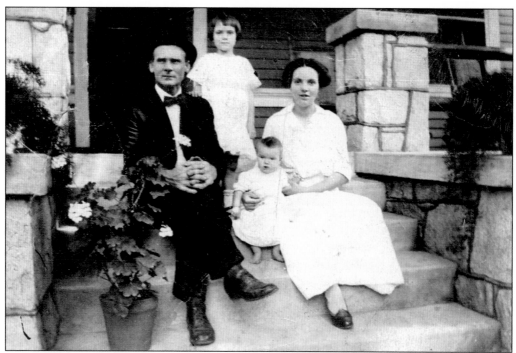

James Lemon Smith (no relation to the Lemon family) married Monnie Turner in 1907. They are photographed at their Dallas Street home in 1913 with Jean and Ann, two of their eight children. Dr. and Mrs. Gene Bailey previously owned this home that featured granite from the Stone Mountain quarry. Lemon Smith was the City's Water and Lights Superintendent from 1915 to 1958. (Anne Smith Nelson and Nancy Smith Maxwell collection.)

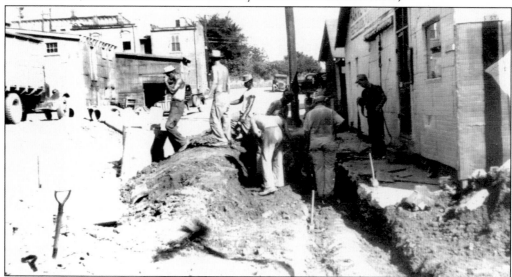

In the late 1940s, Lemon Smith supervised the installation of water and sewer lines throughout the downtown area. In this photograph, pipe is being laid on Center Street (later Senator Russell Square) in front of city buildings, including the fire station with its bell pole. These buildings were later replaced with the Quonset hut that currently houses city hall. (Anne Smith Nelson and Nancy Maxwell Smith collection.)

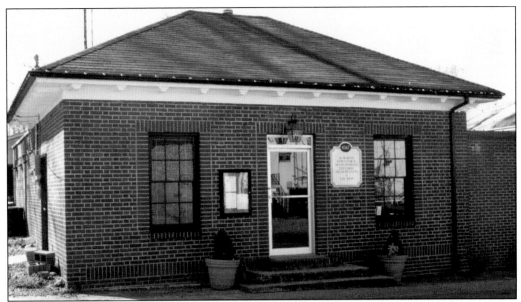

The "most modern calaboose" in Cobb County opened with much fanfare in June 1935, including an open inspection of the building and a barbecue on water works hill. Built for $3,000 with assistance from the Federal Emergency Relief Administration, the new "escape-proof" jail contained six cells and housed the city council room.[12] Used as a jail for over 60 years, the renovated building now houses the city Office of Downtown Development, Historic Preservation and Tourism. (ASHP collection.)

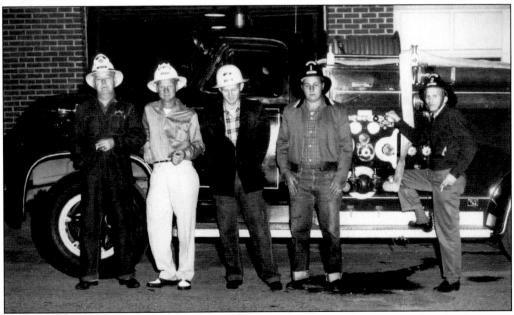

The Acworth Volunteer Fire Department was organized in 1907 by its first fire chief, Eugene W. Ray. Claude Durham and J.E. Carnes were the first company captains. J.C. Jolly, Bill Smith, Hollis Maxwell, Dural Kennedy, and Bob Lyons continued the volunteer tradition here in the mid-1950s. They are standing in front of the Quonset hut that was then used for the fire station and city hall. (Nancy and Hollis Maxwell collection.)

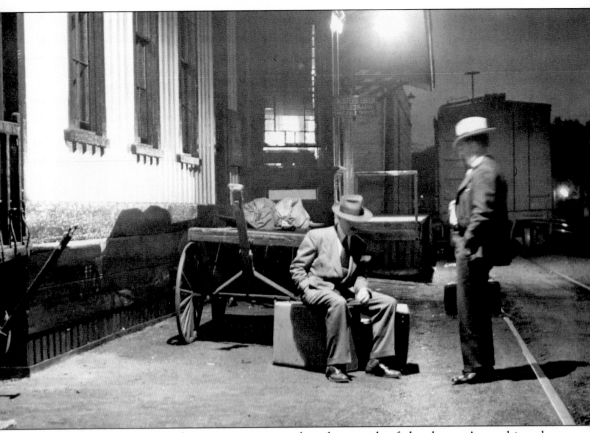

Drummers arrive on the evening train in this photograph of the depot. Acworthians have always been intimate with the sound of a train whistle blowing, rushing to its call in the early days to meet visitors and returning friends. In later years, the line has been reserved exclusively for freight use. Two-thirds of Acworth's 20th-century depot were devoted to freight and one-third to passenger service. In the name of progress in the early 1980s, the depot was cut in half and moved from its Lemon Street location to Winn Street where it remains today. The crossing at Cherokee Street was then closed and a new railroad intersection was created where the depot had stood. (Photo by Fred Kienel.)

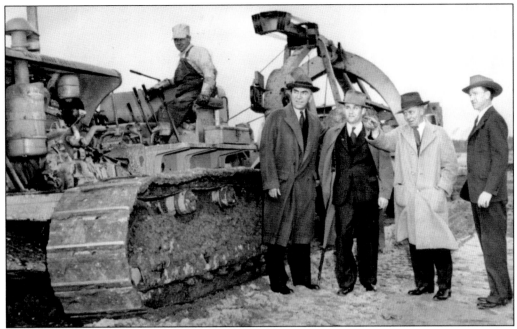

Eddie Rickenbacker, WWI Flying Ace and automobile/airlines magnate, toured southeastern Army Air Corps training bases in 1942. He is standing here on the left with James Carmichael, Cobb County attorney; R.M. Blair, Marietta mayor; and Acworthian George Huie McMillan, Cobb County Commissioner. The three Cobb Countians were instrumental in bringing the Bell Bomber Plant to Rickenbacker Field in Marietta. Its successor today, Lockheed Martin, employs thousands. (Vanishing Georgia collection, Georgia Dept. of Archives and History.)

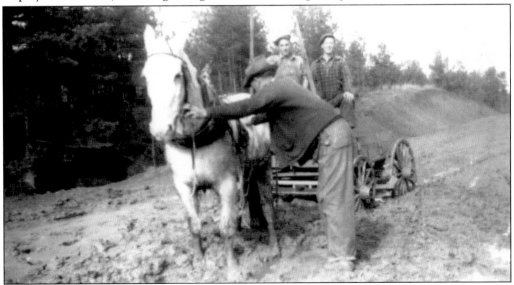

Highway 92 (Lake Acworth Drive) is a muddy mess in this early 1940s photograph. Although the highway was being paved, Cobb County Commissioner McMillan pulled all the county's road equipment to Bell Aircraft Corporation's construction site. With the launch of Bell's huge plant for the production of B-29s for World War II, the rural county was transformed. Cobb's population escalated and industrial growth soared. (Gene Cheatham collection.)

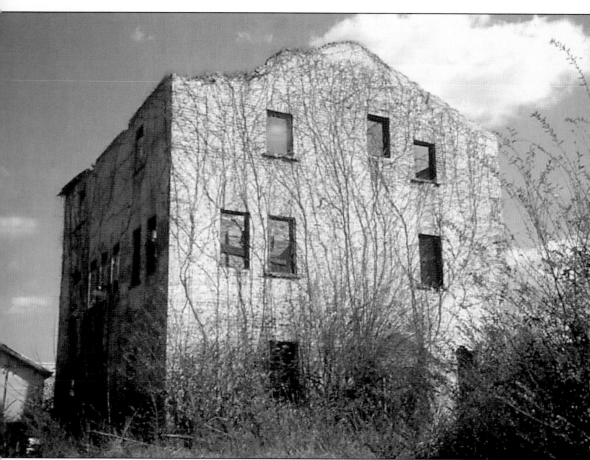

Acworthian John Cowan went west in the 1850s to seek his fortune in Montana's Black Hills. His band of prospectors, the "Four Georgians," is credited with founding Helena and striking gold at their mine, Last Chance Gulch. A decade later Cowan returned to Acworth with a substantial fortune and built this mill with his friends Tarlton Moore and Smith Lemon on present-day Southside Drive on property from the Mitchell estate. This three-story mill was constructed in 1873 of brick and heavy timber frame. It originally output a fine flour, called "lynette," reportedly at a rate of 100 barrels a day. In the 1920s, the structure housed a hosiery mill and then served as a warehouse for a tapestry weaving mill. In later years, this structure was used for storage until a fire destroyed the interior wood floors, beams, and roof in 1993. (ASHP collection.)

Four

MILL TOWN

By the late 1920s, Acworth's three textile mills were in their prime, employing hundreds and producing tapestries, coarse cloths, and hosiery. Acworth's oldest commercial structure on Southside Drive was originally built as a grist mill. In later years, the original mill and more modern manufacturing buildings on the same site were used for producing fine textiles under several owners and names.

Orlando Awtrey founded the Acworth Cotton Manufacturing Company in 1905 on the Kitchen farm. The mill originally produced cotton yarns. With the fashion change from cotton to silk stockings in the 1920s, the mill modified its product.[13] Helen and Esther Sill, two sisters from Connecticut, purchased the mill, invested capital, and manufactured coarse sheetings: tobacco shadecloth, osnaburg, and sacks. Their company, Acworth Mills, employed 200 people. It also provided a whole village for its workers, including homes, a company store, a church, and the Eli Whitney School.

Labor problems in the north were the impetus behind Unique Knitting Company's move from Philadelphia south. Fred Kienel and his hosiery business were lured to Acworth specifically by low taxes, low wages, and free land. The Acworth Board of Trade purchased a cotton field on North Main Street and five acres of the McMillan property adjoining Main Street and Collins Avenue. It then sold the land to Unique for "one dollar and other considerations." Unique constructed the mill on the cotton field and sold the residential land to Fred Kienel personally.

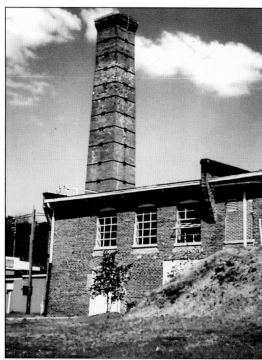

The Sill's business Acworth Mills was sold to the Clark Thread Company. Clark (later Coats and Clark) employed as many as 300 local residents. The mill closed in the 1980s due to foreign textile competition and the lack of sufficient skilled labor. Since 1995 the complex, as photographed here, has housed a printing company. Much of the historic fabric of the mill is still visible, including brick buildings, windows, and water towers. (ASHP collection.)

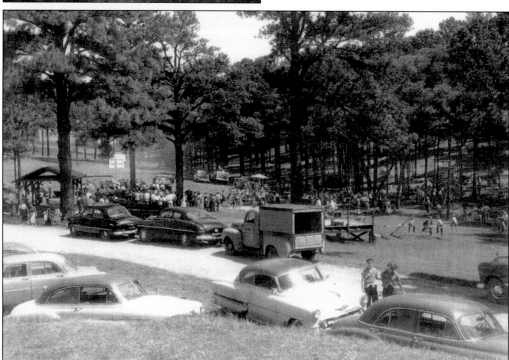

When the Clark Thread Company bought the mill in 1947, it established the village ballfields adjacent to Main Street and made improvements in the housing, streets, and utilities. The company also sponsored an annual picnic for the entire Acworth community. Local folks gather at Coats and Clark field in this photograph from the late 1940s. (Acworth HPC collection.)

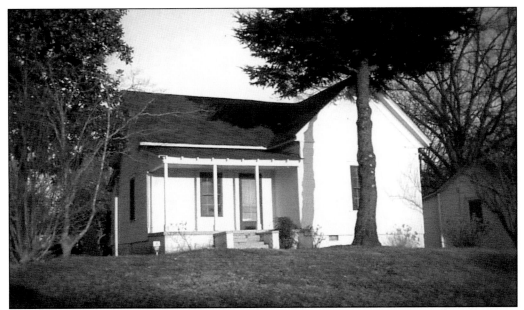

The Mill Village encompasses about 55 homes on 54 acres on Thomasville, Clarkdale, and Toccoa Drives. In the 1920s a mill home rented for 50¢ a week, which included water, sewer, and garbage service. There were four styles of homes from most common to least: pyramidal (often a duplex), side-gabled, gabled-ell (shown here), and shotgun. The mill homes were sold to private owners in late 1960s. (ASHP collection.)

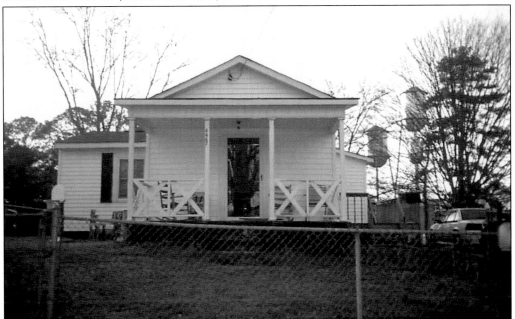

The Mill Village houses were originally constructed with brick pier foundations, wood clapboard siding, and standing-seam metal roofs. Coats and Clark renovated the houses in the late 1940s. The open foundations were filled with concrete block, the roofs were changed to asphalt shingle, and the clapboard was replaced with asbestos siding. The form of many of the homes, like this shotgun, remain unchanged today. (ASHP collection.)

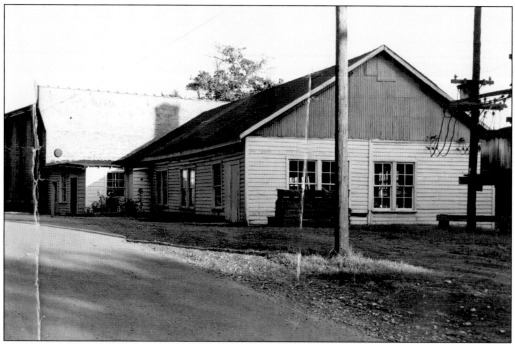

Operators of the original Cowan mill site pictured here on Southside Drive included Acworth Hosiery Mills (1921), Elizabeth Bartlett Mills (1928), Cherokee Mills (1939), Rothschild Mills (1941), and Americo (1985). Starting with the Bartlett Mills, heavy weave fabrics were produced for bedspreads, tapestries, upholstery, and draperies. (Acworth HPC collection.)

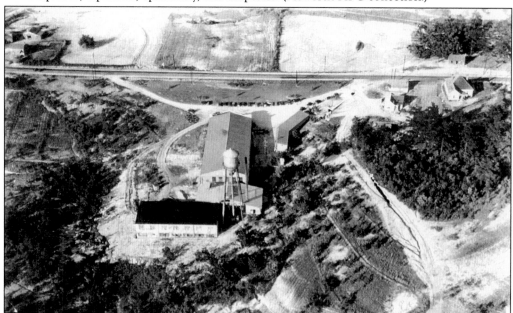

Fred Kienel of Philadelphia moved to Acworth in 1926 to establish the Unique Knitting mill. He scouted out factory sites in Georgia and was persuaded to build on North Main Street by the Acworth Board of Trade. This aerial view from the 1930s shows the improvements to the site from the original 65-by-165-foot building. (Robert J. Kienel collection.)

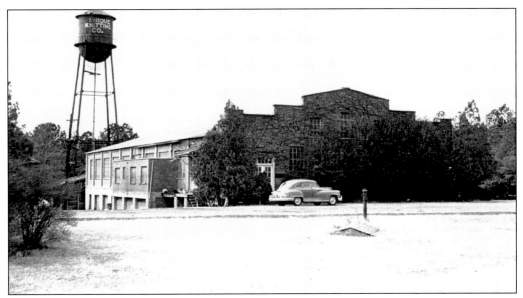

Unique was founded by Kienel's grandfather in 1908 in Philadelphia. It manufactured dress and athletic tube socks and employed about 150 locals for the 55 years of its existence in Acworth. Unique's weekly output ranged from 5,000 dozen pairs of socks in its early years to 10,000 in later years. In 1940 the front facade was updated as shown here. (Robert J. Kienel collection.)

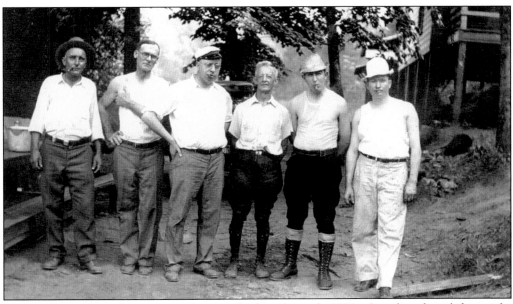

Unique Knitting employees were photographed in the early 1930s. Standing from left to right are unidentified, Lemon Smith Sr., Fred Kienel, George Louden, and two unidentified people. Fred Kienel and his wife moved to Acworth with their four young children, Alma, Buddy, Joe, and Bob. Mrs. Kienel died of typhoid about one year later. Mr. Kienel later remarried Georgia Gholston, a teacher from Atlanta. (Robert J. Kienel collection.)

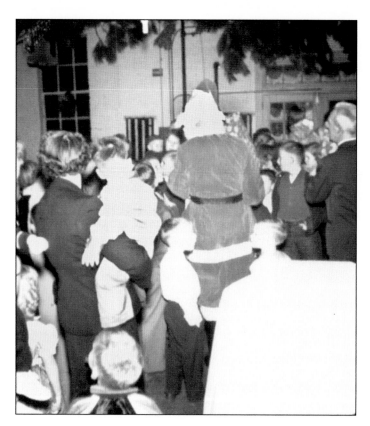

Unique workers and children celebrate at a company Christmas party complete with a visit from Santa Claus. About 65 to 70 percent of the employees were women. (Robert J. Kienel collection.)

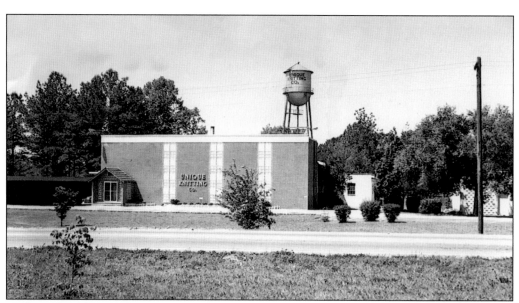

In the 1960s, the new brick office building shown here was built fronting Main Street. At this time, Unique was operating three shifts, six days a week. (Robert J. Kienel collection.)

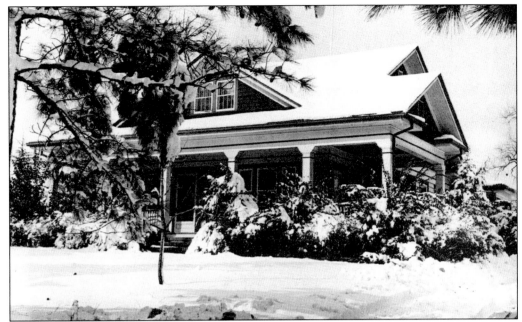

The Kienel compound contained four Craftsman bungalows, including Fred Kienel's personal residence pictured here. The houses featured modern, open floor plans. The porte-cochere of this house attested to the important emergence of the automobile in the late 1920s and the freedom it gave owners and managers to live offsite from the mill. The compound remained intact until Fred Kienel's death in 1982. (Robert J. Kienel collection.)

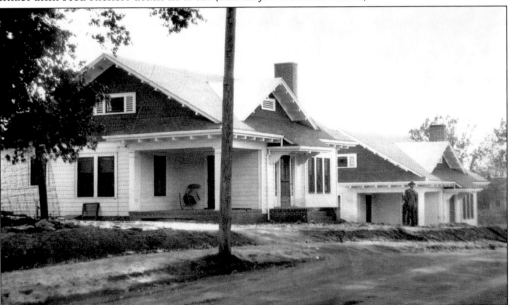

The two smaller Kienel bungalows facing Collins Avenue were reserved for managers at the mill. Both homes have had the porches enclosed and other modifications made to the original three-bedroom, one-bath homes. All of the homes were based on designs by Leila Ross Wilburn, a noted Atlanta architect and female pioneer in her field. Opening her office in 1909, Wilburn exclusively designed residential properties. (Dene Sheheane Collection.)

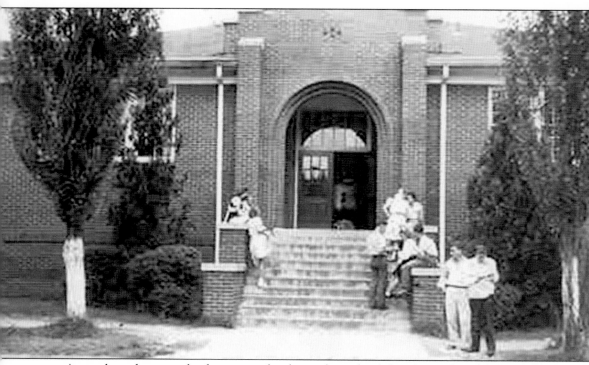

Acworth students on the front steps finish another school day. Acworth School served as an inclusive primary and high school until 1957 when North Cobb High School was built. The new Bernard Awtrey Middle School eventually siphoned off grades six, seven, and eight. Acworth School then served as an elementary school with grades kindergarten through five until the new elementary school on Cantrell Road opened in 2001. (1940 Acworth School Annual.)

Five

SCHOOL DAYS

The pioneer town of Acworth had a school for its children as early as 1852. Nathan W. Smith was reportedly one of the first teachers. The site at Academy Street and Dixie Avenue had housed a school since at least 1868 on land donated by Smith Lemon. Early school terms ran from January to March and July to September in accordance with the needs of the farming calendar.

In 1899, the Acworth School became the Smith-Lemon Institute, a chartered school. It is unclear why the name change occurred but it is speculated that the town hoped to attract quality scholars and funds. The school continued to be known by either name and included grades one through eleven. It was recognized as top-notch, and Acworth was one of the smallest towns in Georgia with an accredited school. Other grammar schools fed into Acworth High School including Mars Hill, Allatoona, Hickory Grove, and Eli Whitney. Acworth ran its own school system until 1935 when it consolidated with Cobb County Schools.

Until 1967, black Acworthians were schooled separately from their white counterparts. A two-story Masonic lodge behind School Street served as an early grammar school. In the 1920s, it was supplanted by a Rosenwald School. Julius Rosenwald, a Jewish philanthropist and Sears president, donated millions of dollars in seed money for the creation of black schools in the South, with communities matching one-half of the costs. The Rosenwald school was replaced on the same site by Roberts School in the 1950s. Acworth did not have a black high school. Early scholars had to find their own way to Atlanta's Booker T. Washington High School. Later students were bused to Lemon Street High School in Marietta.

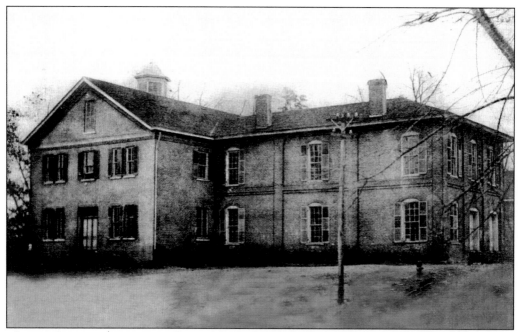

The Smith-Lemon Institute is photographed c. 1900 looking south down Academy Street. The building was a two-story, front-facing, gabled T plan. The building that housed the institute was razed in the 1930s to make way for a new school building on the same grounds but parallel to Dixie Avenue. (Acworth HPC collection.)

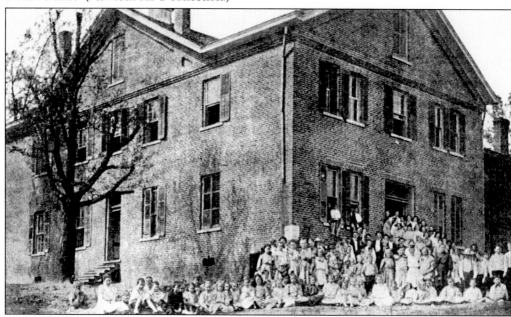

This view of the Smith-Lemon Institute shows students outside the back of the building facing the school grounds. The institute accepted both local and boarding students in grades one through eleven. Students boarded with local families. The institute had different courses of study including Collegiate and Christian ministry. Candidates for the Christian ministry did not pay tuition.[14] (Acworth HPC collection.)

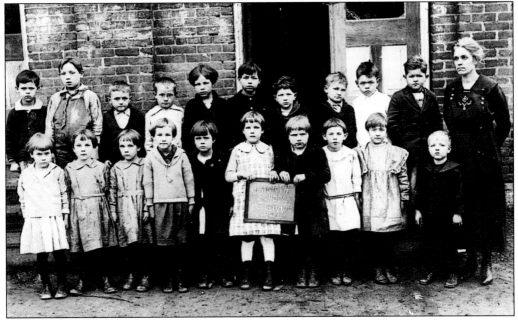

Pascal McLain was a product of the Acworth school system. He is pictured here with his first-grade class in 1922. (Pascal McLain collection.)

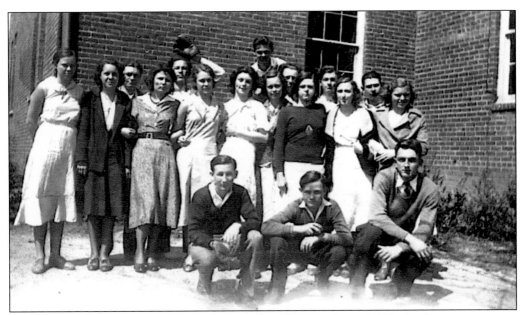

Pascal McLain posed with his Acworth School graduating class of 1932. At this time, in-town students paid tuition to attend Acworth High School; tuition for out-of-town students was paid for by Cobb County. Pascal McLain and his classmates went through the 11th grade. The 12th grade was not added until 1955. (Pascal McLain collection.)

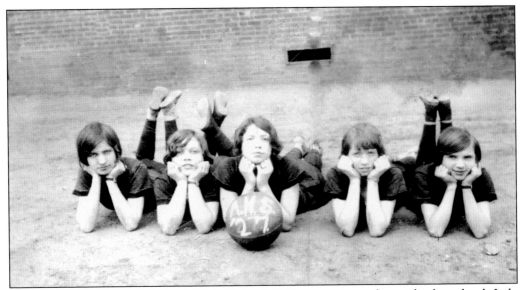

The 1927 Acworth High School Girls Basketball Team is pictured outside the school. Lola Collins Swanson Gray is right behind the basketball. (McCoy family collection.)

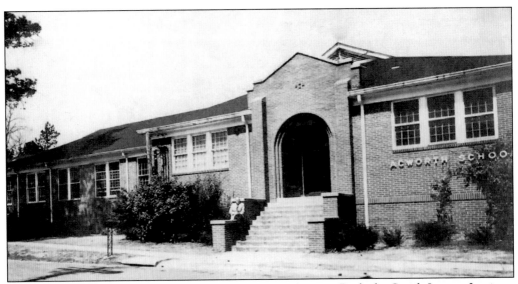

The new Acworth School was built in 1936 on Dixie Avenue. Both the Smith-Lemon Institute and the original Acworth Methodist Church buildings were razed for the new construction. The old church building had been used by the school for classroom space and as a gymnasium after the church had moved to its new building on Main Street in 1905. (Roy McClure collection.)

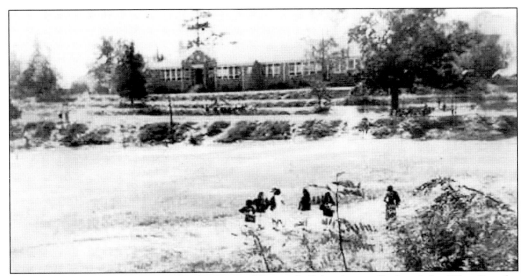

As evidenced by this photograph, the front of Acworth School actually faced the "Flats," as the grounds were known. Football games, track meets, baseball games, and other sporting events took place here. (Sandra Newberry Teague collection.)

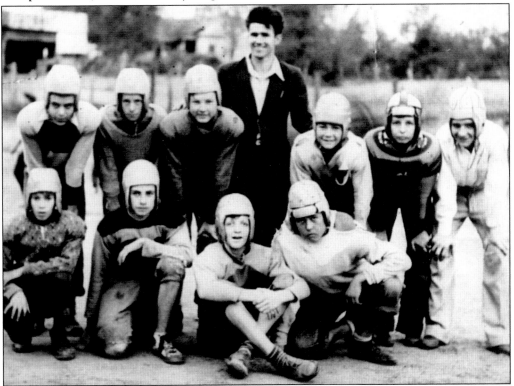

In 1937 the Acworth "Skullbusters" football team played on the "Flats," and won three games, tied one, and lost four. Photographed from left to right are (front row) Lloyd Ingram, James Rainey, Bob Kienel, and Capt. Grady Gee; (back row) Robert Clark, ? Turner, Evans Winn, Coach Clymmis McKinney or "Mac," Glen Reed, George Hadaway, and James Lemon Smith Jr. or "Red." (Robert M. Clark collection.)

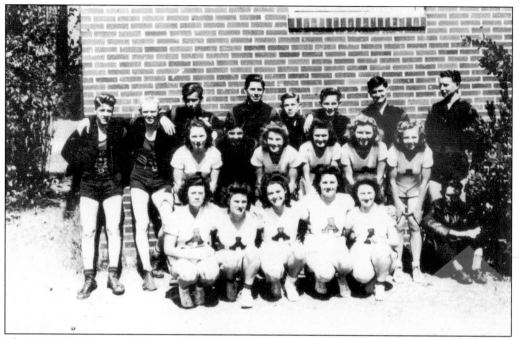

The 1942–1943 Acworth Boys and Girls basketball teams are photographed outside the school. (Roy McClure collection.)

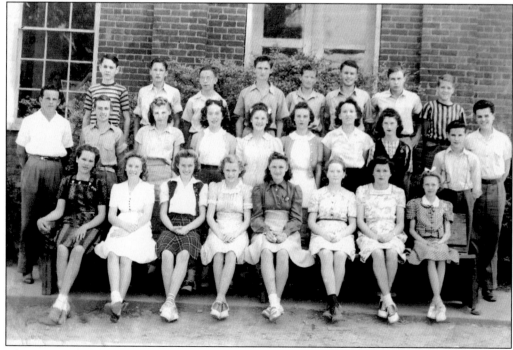

The 1942 and 1943 Acworth High School graduates included members of the Ruff, Hufstetler, Pope, Ford, Walker, Patrick, Shinall, Ehlert, Nation, Rainey, Grogan, Cantrell, Smith, Spiegel, McCoy, Hester, Clark, Guess, Mason, Hembree, Tumlin, Pitner, Hadaway, and Kemp families. (Beth Watson collection.)

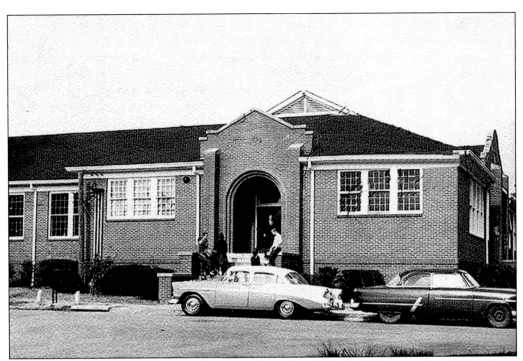

Students socialize on the side steps of Acworth School in 1960. By 1950, more than 300 students attended Acworth High School; over 500 students were in the grammar school.[15] (1960 Acworth School Annual.)

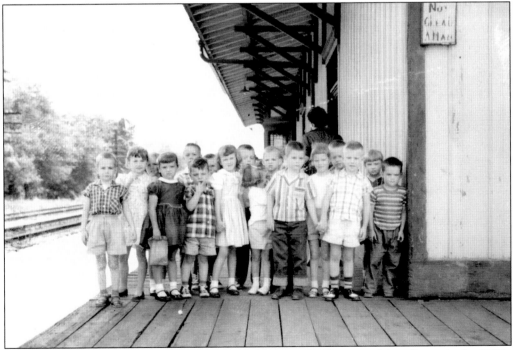

Hartley Grey's Acworth class took a walking field trip to the Depot on Main Street in the 1950s. (McCoy family collection.)

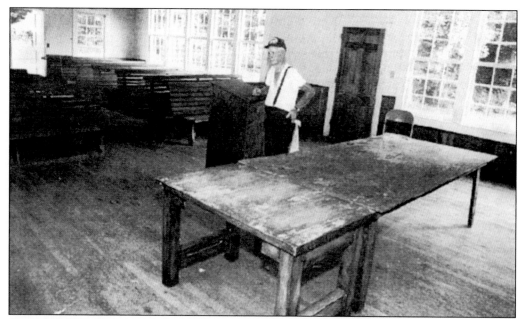

Caretaker W.C. Skinner stands in the interior of the one-room Mars Hill Schoolhouse, adjacent to the Mars Hill cemetery. The cemetery dates to 1841; the school building, the second on the site, was built in 1883 on land donated by James Lile Lemon. At one time the interior walls were painted as a blackboard due to the scarcity of slate. Students ranged in age from 6 to 16. (Odene Rakestraw collection.)

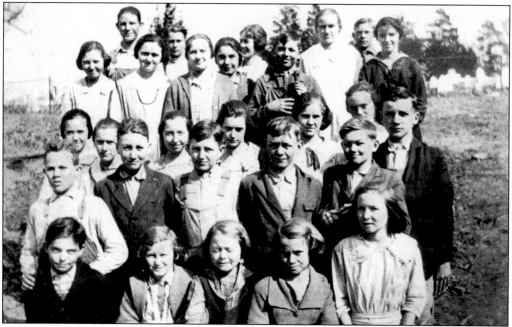

Mars Hill grammar school students gathered for a group photo in the early 1920s. Inez Scroggs is in the front row, second from the right. She later married Earle Awtrey, son of Orlando Awtrey Sr. One longtime educator, George McMillan Orr, taught school here from 1895 to 1918. (Reginald Awtrey Collection.)

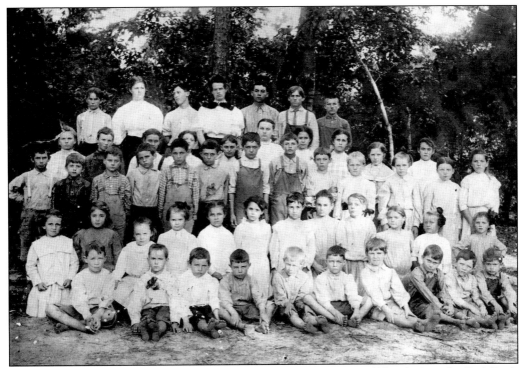

Allatoona School was located on County Line Road past Mars Hill but before the Red Rock community. This group photographed in 1906 included A.E. Brown and three Pitner boys: John Gordon, Clyde Thomas, and Clarence W. (Hinton Brown collection.)

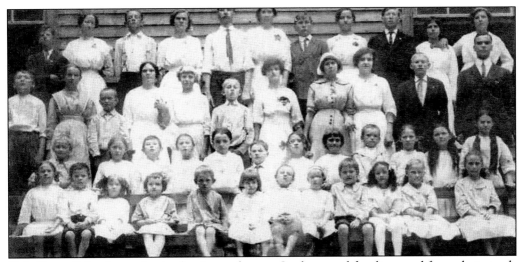

Oak Grove School was also in the Acworth area. Students and faculty posed for a photograph in 1913. (Roy McClure collection.)

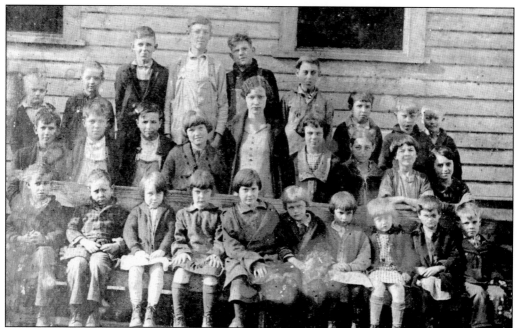

Awtrey School was located on Awtrey Church Road. Students are pictured outside the school in the 1930s. (Elizabeth Hufstetler Craig.)

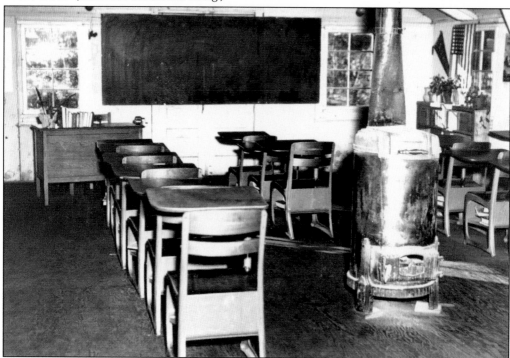

Eli Whitney School served the Acworth Mill Village children from 1928 until 1947 as part of the Cobb County school system. This interior photo depicts one of the 1930s classrooms complete with a coal-burning stove. After 1947 the school was used as a community house for the mill village. (Vanishing Georgia collection, Georgia Dept. of Archives and History.)

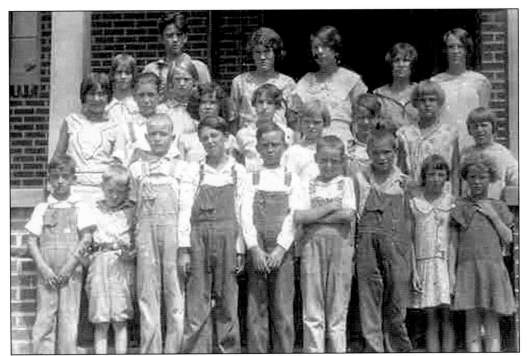

Some of the Eli Whitney students were photographed in front of the school in the early 1930s, including children from the Jones, Cantrell, Graham, Dover, Green, Haynes, McPherson, Peterson, Fowler, Brackett, Lanning, Waller, Lang, and Crawford families. (Esteen Jones collection.)

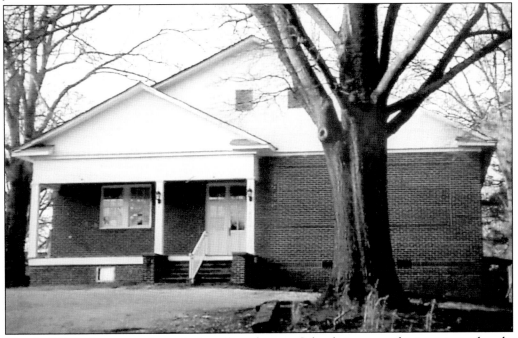

The building that once housed the Eli Whitney School is currently in private hands. (ASHP collection.)

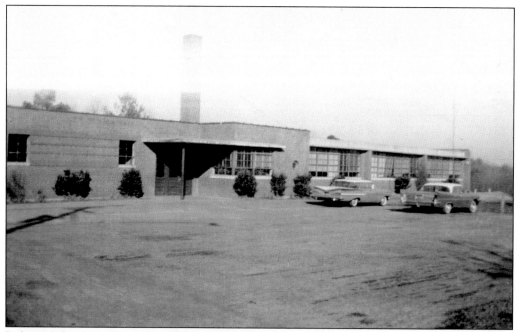

Roberts School was located on School Street in the late 1950s. After schools were integrated in Cobb County in 1967, the building housed the City's Public Works and Water Departments and the Cobb County Health Department. (Tim Houston collection.)

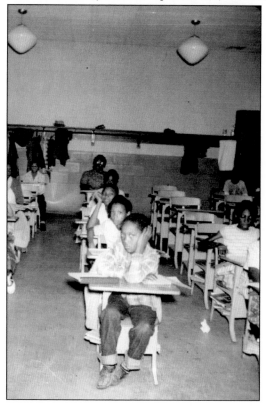

An interior shot shows a Roberts School classroom from the late 1950s. Some of the families who sent their children here included Blaylock, Gragg, Houston, Griffin, Byrd, Mitchell, Hill, and Morris. (Tim Houston collection.)

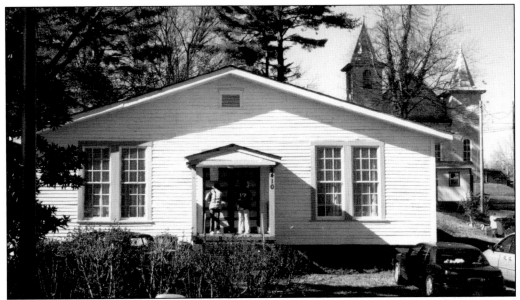

The Rosenwald school was torn down from its School Street location and rebuilt board by board on Cherokee Street in the late 1940s/early 1950s. As illustrated in this current photograph, it was a typical Rosenwald design—wood with large banks of windows. It was given to the neighborhood for use as a community center. Children had to attend school at Bethel or Zion Hill Churches until Roberts School was completed in the 1950s. (ASHP collection.)

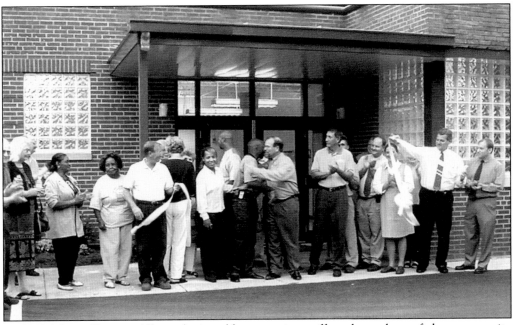

In 2002 Mayor Tommy Allegood, city aldermen, city staff, and members of the community cut the ribbon for the new Roberts School. Community Development Block Grants and the City of Acworth provided funding for its renovation into a community center. The community and city will work together to provide after-school programs and other classes here. (Photo by Daniel Timmons.)

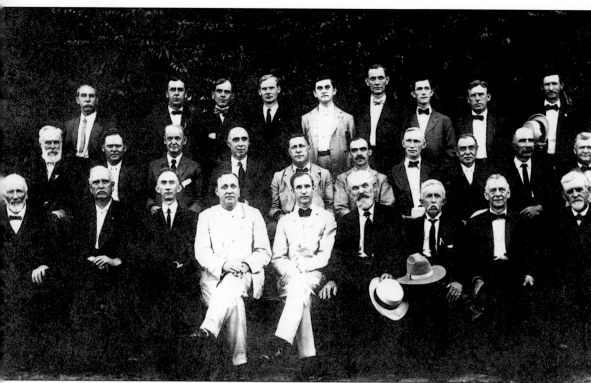

A tent was pitched on the vacant lot on Lemon Street behind the Acworth Inn for a three-week evangelistic meeting of the Churches of Acworth, c. 1915. W.S. Northcutt recalled Methodist minister Charles Bass preaching that the Devil came through Acworth every day on the Dixie Flyer train but saw so much meanness he didn't bother to get off.[16] Bass-Stapleton meeting participants, pictured from left to right, are (front row) Rev. ? Hughes, Rev. A.J. Morgan, Rev. E.D. Patton, Rev. Charles Bass, Mr. Stapleton, Rev. M.A. McCoy, unidentified, Penn Mitchell, and J.F. Collins; (middle row) J.N. Johnson, Dr. W.C. Burtz, Col. J.J. Northcutt, R.L. McMillan, Dr. W.C. Humphries, J.E. Carnes, W.M. Webb, W.L. Abbott, G.W. McMillan, and Dr. E.M. Bailey; (back row) Lucius Rainey, Lester Pyron, Rogers Lemon, J. Lemon Smith, F.G. Hull, Fate Swanson, Mr. ? Grogan, W.H. Tanner, George McLain, and Pete McLain. (Acworth HPC collection.)

Six

SUNDAY BEST

The core of the Acworth community is in its churches. The prominent town churches all date to the mid-19th century and most of their buildings date to before the turn of that century. Relationships between the churches were often collaborative. In the years before the Civil War and immediately after, the Methodists, Presbyterians, and Christians held a "Union Sunday School" because each had too few members for separate instruction. After the Christian Church burned in 1899, Acworth Baptist Church extended the use of its building for worship until the church could be rebuilt.

Around 1915 the churches sponsored a three-week evangelistic meeting. The Bass-Stapleton assembly led to the creation of a union prayer meeting on Wednesday nights that alternated from church to church. It also resulted in the establishment of the Acworth Evangelistic Club, an interdenominational organization aiming to promote fellowship and good works in the community.

Two very strong black churches have existed in Acworth since the early days of emancipation: Zion Hill Baptist Church and Bethel African Methodist Episcopal Church. The first congregations of both churches shared a building, meeting alternate Sundays with community members attending at each. Even after each church had acquired its own building, the alternating services continued. The Bethel A.M.E. Church, probably the least changed of all the Acworth churches, is on the National and Acworth Historic Registers.

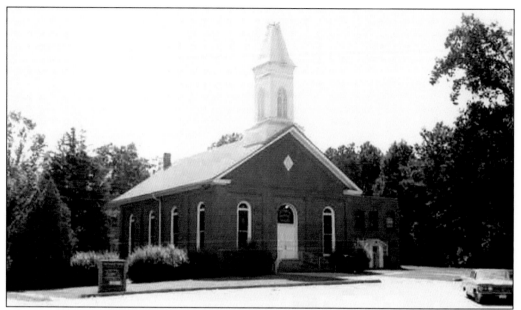

The Liberty Hill Baptist Church was organized in 1840. It was housed in a log structure near Liberty Hill Cemetery. Destroyed by Sherman's troops, the church was rebuilt in 1866. In 1872, the present building on Main Street was constructed and the name was changed from Liberty Hill to Acworth Baptist. The church has been enlarged and renovated over the years; this photo shows it before the 1967 remodel. (Roy McClure collection.)

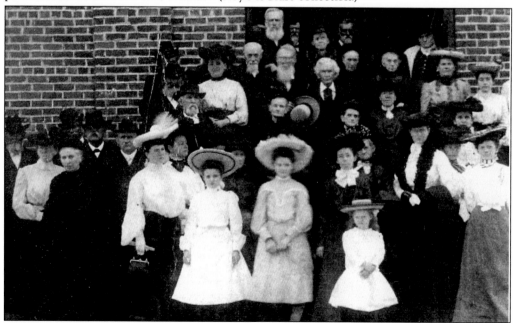

Members of the Acworth Baptist Church gathered outside for a photograph c. 1910. Mary Ann Sims and husband Hiram Anderson Butler are fourth and fifth from the left. Mr. Butler worked for the railroad for over 40 years and helped capture Andrews's raiders in the chase of "The General." The Bates sisters, Julia and Lou, are in the light dresses in the front. (Mimi Jo Butler collection.)

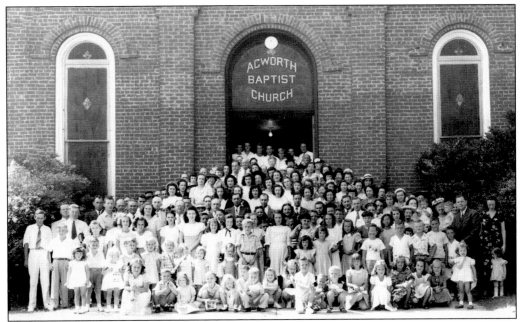

First Baptist Church of Acworth (name adopted in 1946) members are pictured in the late 1940s, including then-pastor A.C. Stephens and his wife. The first charter members included the John Collinses, the Cargill Drakes, the L.W. Ginns, Daniel Collins, and W.R. Graham. (Shirley Fowler Walker collection.)

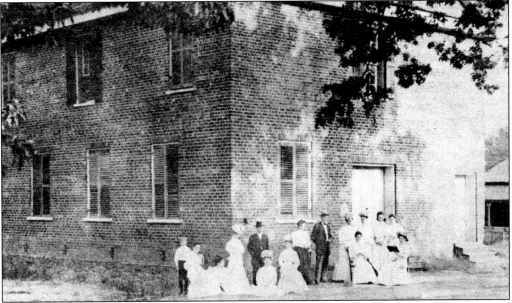

The Acworth Methodist Church was organized in 1858. The first church, pictured here, was constructed in 1859 on the corner of Academy Street and Dixie Avenue adjacent to the Acworth School. The land was donated to the church with the instruction that the second floor be reserved for a Masonic Lodge. The building served as a hospital during the Civil War. When it was razed for the construction of the new Acworth School in 1936, human bones, buttons, and other Civil War relics were reportedly found. (Robert M. Clark collection.)

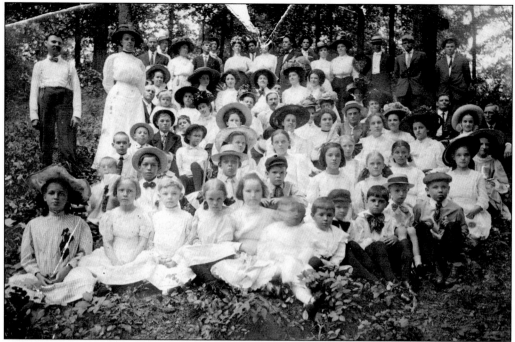

A Methodist Sunday school photograph dates from the early 20th century. (Robert M. Clark collection.)

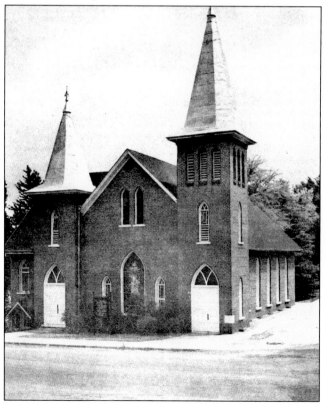

A second Methodist church was constructed at Main Street and Morningside Drive in 1905 at a cost of $3,500. That structure photographed here survived until the 1980s. Frana Brown Park, named after a longtime city clerk, now occupies its space and contains its cornerstone and bell. In 1957, having outgrown the building, the church acquired seven acres from the Army Corps of Engineers and built a third church on Lake Acworth Drive. (Robert M. Clark collection.)

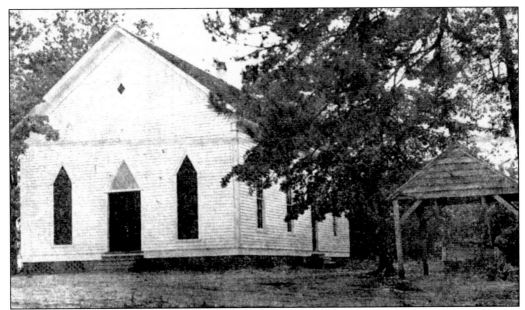

The Mars Hill Presbyterian Church was organized in 1837 by charter members Thomas and Rachel McEver, Margaret Eccles, George and Sarah McMillan, John and Elizabeth Orr, and Phebe Wigley. The original church building was on a knoll behind Mars Hill Cemetery (where Mars Hill School would later be located). The church photographed here was erected after the Civil War and bricked in 1953. (Odene Rakestraw collection.)

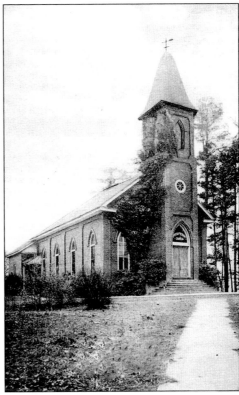

The Acworth Presbyterian Church was established in 1870 as a mission from the Mars Hill Church. Thirty-four members were dispatched to start the Acworth Church, and Mars Hill provided a joint minister until 1956. Smith Lemon donated the property and, together with his brother James Lile, supervised the construction of the church building in 1875. The building has experienced few architectural changes over the years as evidenced by this 1962 postcard. (Reginald Awtrey Collection.)

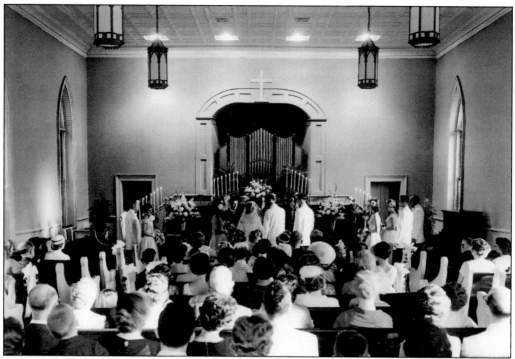

Suzanne McMillan's wedding in 1959 provides an interior shot of the Acworth Presbyterian Church. (Jane McMillan Baird collection.)

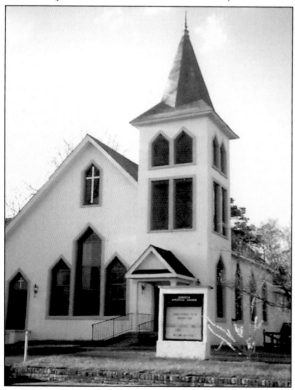

The Christian Church was organized in 1858 as the Mount Zion Church of Christ and met in a frame building on Mitchell Hill. It was destroyed by Union troops during the Civil War. The federal government later reimbursed the church for its loss. In 1877 Nathan Smith helped to reorganize and build a new church at Northside Drive and School Street. That building burned in 1899. The present structure shown here in a current photograph was erected in 1901. (ASHP collection.)

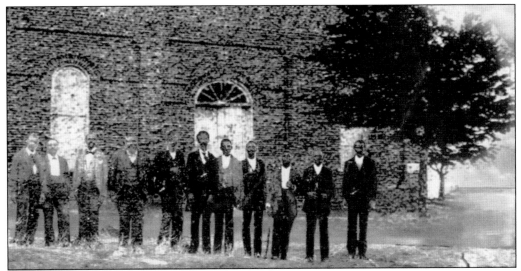

The Bethel A.M.E. Church was formed in 1864 by former slaves. Trustees reportedly included George McConnell, Benjamin Davenport, Mitchell Saddler, John Buffington, Wyeth (Wyatt) Dobbs, Henry Hesterly, Ezekiel Buffington, and Peter Carter. The property was either purchased from L.L. Robertson or Col. E.L. and Kate Shuford. The sanctuary of the church was built between 1871 and 1882. This photo shows congregants in front of the church on Bell Street before modification. (Acworth HPC collection.)

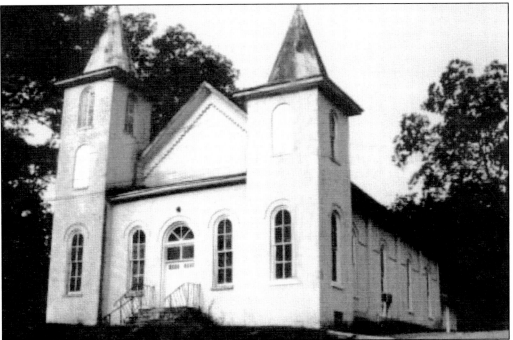

This view of Bethel shows the 1895 addition of the vestibule and two towers during J.R. Fleming's tenure. Pastor Fleming was assigned to several churches in Georgia and helped to erect a church in Stone Mountain. The R. Nelson named as the contractor on the cornerstone is presumed to be Robert Nelson, a brick mason born in 1856. He and his wife, Victoria, had one son, Charles, who was also a brick mason. (Acworth HPC collection.)

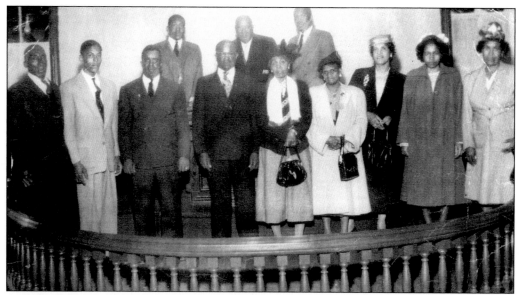

An interior shot of the church shows the original balustrade. The Romanesque Revival church has also retained the original interior beaded, tongue-and-groove coffered ceiling and the pulpit. Members of the church photographed here in 1949, from left to right, are (front row) Belton Payton, George Thomas Rice, Ernest Morris, Cisrow Talley, Era Bell McConnell, Sally Floyd, Mosie Roberts, Annie Lee Lewis, and Odessa Henderson; (back row) two unidentified people and Rev. Sim Lewis. (Acworth HPC collection.)

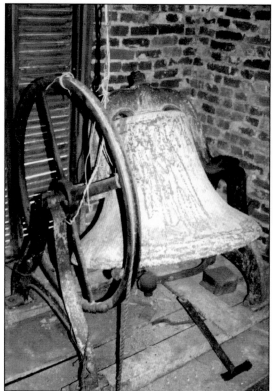

The Bethel A.M.E. Church cast iron bell is probably original to the bell tower construction in 1895; bells of this large size (33 1/4 inches in diameter) have not been cast since the late 1940s. The bell has served not only to call the faithful to worship, but also as the neighborhood fire alarm. (Acworth HPC collection.)

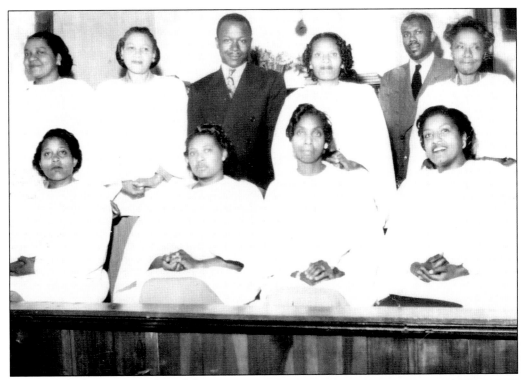

The Bethel Choir in 1949, from left to right, included (front row) Katherine Grissom, Eulah Morris, Mary Lee Cooper, and Anna Lou Cole; (back row) Evelyn Taylor, Mamie Young, Amos Durr, Reba Henderson, Rev. Sim Lewis, and Annie Lee Payton. (Acworth HPC collection.)

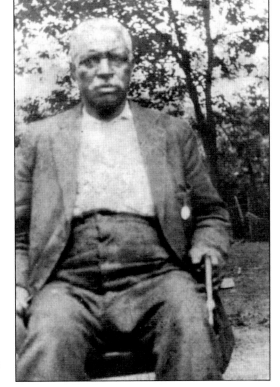

Wiley Gragg was a longtime member of Bethel who came to Acworth as a young man in the late 1800s. He first worked as a farmer, then as a meat cutter for Peter McLain's meat market. He reportedly learned to slaughter meat on the Tippen farm. He was known to slaughter a steer on a Saturday morning and drive through town selling cuts. (Evelyn Gragg collection.)

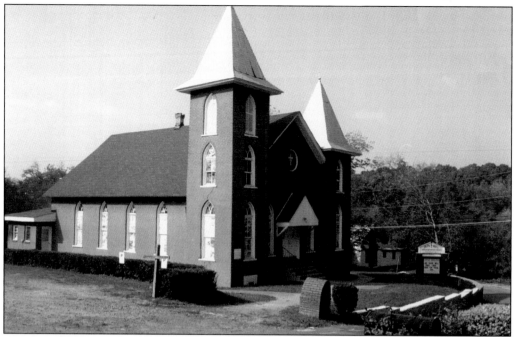

The Zion Hill Baptist Church congregation also dates to 1864. The church shown here on Taylor Street was built in 1914 under the leadership of Rev. S.H. Jackson and opened its doors without debt. Like the Bethel Church, it was built in the Romanesque Revival style with asymmetrical front towers, simple detailing, and rounded arched windows and door openings. The baptismal pool is in the side yard. (ASHP collection.)

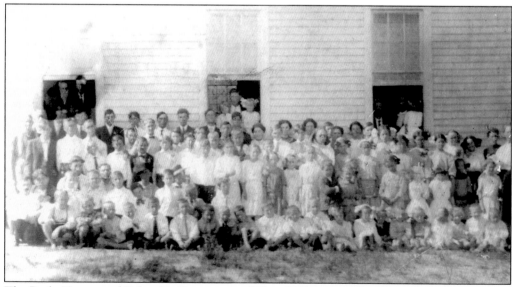

The Bush, House, and Baker families organized Flint Hill Baptist Church in 1877. Ezra Stephen Baker deeded one acre to the Deacons for a church. The church name was changed in 1886 to Hickory Grove. There may have been an earlier church on the site but the present structure on Hickory Grove Road was built in 1910–1911. This photograph shows members gathered in front of the wood-framed church; it was bricked in 1972. (Lil Prather collection.)

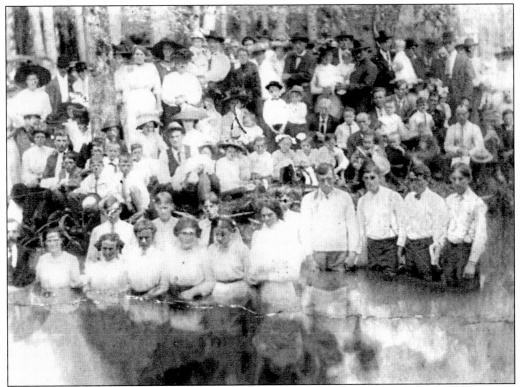

Winn Creek was the site of a Hickory Grove Baptist Church baptism. Members of the Baker family were in attendance. (Lil Prather collection.)

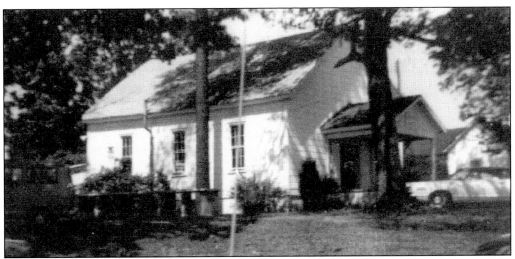

The church on South Main Street was built to serve the mill workers and hosted services for Baptist and Methodist denominations. Dr. Gene Bailey taught Sunday school here. It later became the Shady Grove Baptist Church. The church building shown here no longer exists. (Sandra Newberry Teague collection.)

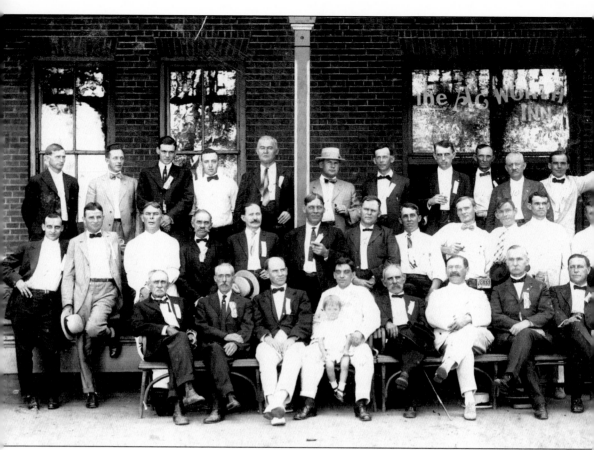

This c. 1915 photograph showcases a classic example of a common social custom of that era—the all-male barbecue smoker, as is evident with many smoking cigars and cigar boxes prominently displayed. Gathered on the veranda of the Acworth Inn are members of Acworth's Masonic Lodge. From left to right are (front row) unidentified, ? West, James W. McMillan, Joe Abbott, Bird Rainey, unidentified, Prof. ? Calvin, and Dr. ? Will; (middle row) ? Abbott, Ernest Collins, Dan Stewart, unidentified, Dr. A.J. Durham, unidentified, Dr. C.W. Burtz, Paul Weldon, Lemon Smith, Lemon Awtrey, and two unidentified; (back row) Jim Riley, unidentified, Hugh Watson, Roy Tippin, unidentified, Howard Crew, two unidentified, J. Glenn Lewis of Kennesaw, unidentified, and Rogers Lemon. (Willie B. Kemp collection.)

Seven

AT PLAY

Early Acworthians enjoyed many diversions including visits, picnics, parties, and trips. Sundays after church were typically reserved for leisure activities. The Awtreys, one of Acworth's earliest families, were well known for social gatherings and merrymaking. Local legend relates that a favorite pastime of Orlando Awtrey was to hitch his horse to his surrey, load the neighborhood children aboard, and spend his day of rest at Moore's Mill. Short train trips were also pleasurable with Atlanta, Marietta, Cartersville, and Kingston as popular destinations.

Before the turn of the 19th century, Acworth was also an appealing destination for summer boarders who enjoyed the Acworth Inn and the relatively cooler weather compared to their homes further south. A mineral well on the corner of Main and Park Streets attracted additional visitors. The hotel was also a popular place for locals to meet, greet train visitors, and gossip. In the Dixie Highway era, Acworthians enjoyed soda fountains, diners, the bowling alley, the movie theater, and a ride about town in their automobiles.

With the damming of the Etowah River and the formation of Lake Allatoona, Acworth seized the opportunity to create a leisure area close to home. City leaders feared Lake Allatoona would be a muddy swamp at the low Acworth end. Therefore, a delegation led by George Huie McMillan went to Washington, D.C. and lobbied for a second, "little dam" to give Acworth year-round recreational water. Acworth's sandy beach featuring a sliding board, train rides, miniature golf, and horseback rides, and its fresh lake water for swimming, boating, and water skiing became regional attractions in the 1950s.

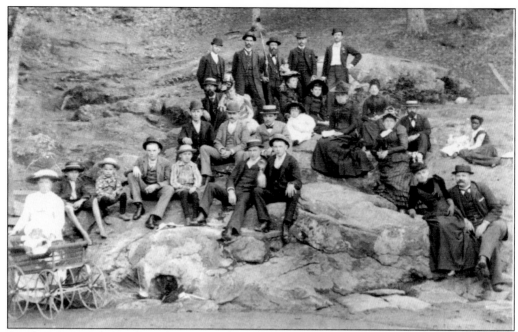

Sunday afternoon picnickers enjoy water from a fresh spring on the rocky banks near Moore's Mill in the early 1900s. Signs of times long past include the collection of communal dipping ladles by the spring at the forefront, a bearded fellow in the rear with his rifle at ready, plus babes in arms and carriages with nursemaids nearby. (Vanishing Georgia collection, Georgia Dept. of Archives and History.)

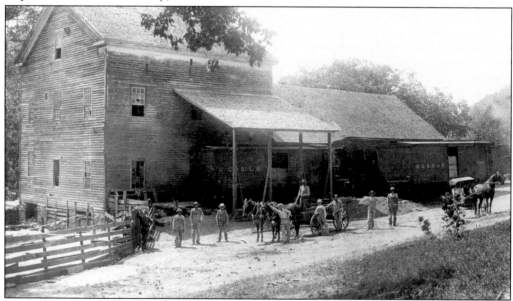

Situated along Pumpkinvine Creek between Acworth and Emerson, Moore's Mill offered local farmers an opportunity to grind corn and flour and have their lumber sawn. Seen in this early photograph is Ensley McCoy (1879–1966) standing second from the left with both hands on his hips. Sparks from the steam engine at the mill are believed to have started the fire that destroyed the structure. (McCoy family collection.)

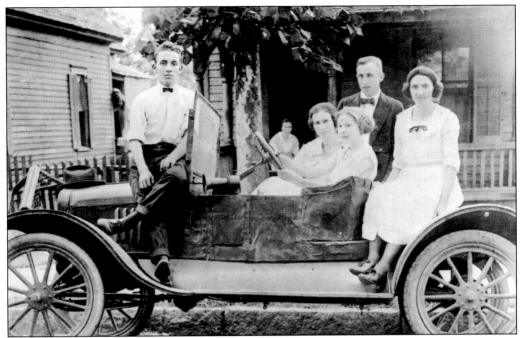

Ernest McClure and Otis Braswell with friends in this 1915 photograph are out for a "turn about town," a popular pastime for the youth of Acworth with the novelty of automobiles. (Vanishing Georgia collection, Georgia Dept. of Archives and History.)

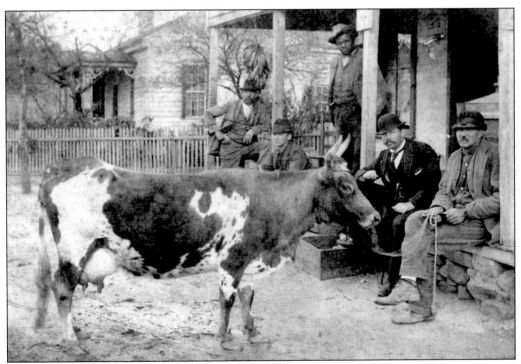

The inclusion of a milk cow in the photo depicts the early rural life in Acworth, as does the variety of attire worn by the men. (Mark Lemon collection.)

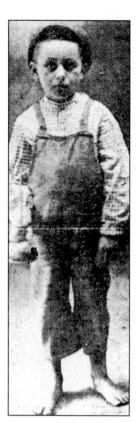

This 1908 photograph appeared in the local newspaper where Master Edward Fowler, at the age of seven years, was dubbed "the youngest engineer in this part of the country." Ed was raised west of Acworth at Proctor's Bend, present-day Galt's Ferry. The farm property included a ginnery and a sawmill that was run on steam, the source of young Ed's engineering prowess. Fowler later served as city alderman and was a member of Acworth Baptist Church and a Mason. (Shirley Fowler Walker collection.)

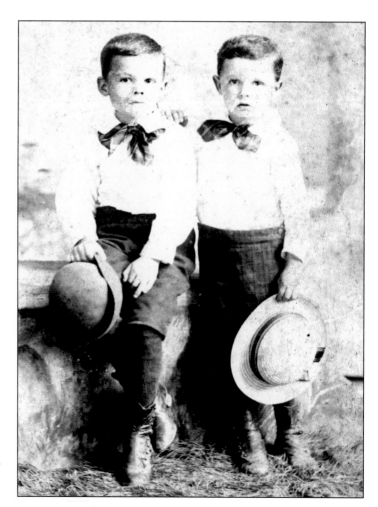

The two sons of Jesse and Lizzie Lemon posed for a portrait in this turn-of-the-19th-century photograph. (Mark Lemon collection.)

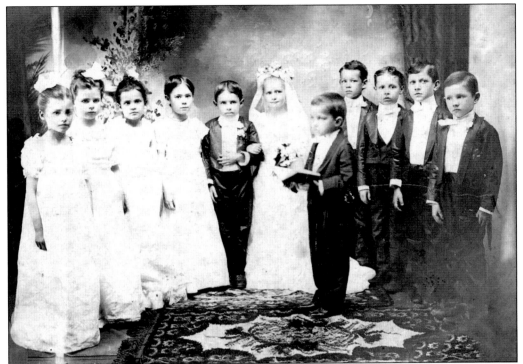

This 1905 photograph of an Acworth Tom Thumb wedding captures, from left to right, young child Scroggins, Lynette Awtrey, unidentified, Elizabeth McMillan, groom Coon Lemon, bride Floy Edwards, young preacher Leonard Stokely, Walter Abbott, Leonard Greene, Lou Rainey, and Richard Tapp. Weddings of this nature were very popular in the days when the circus came to town every year. (Reginald Awtrey collection.)

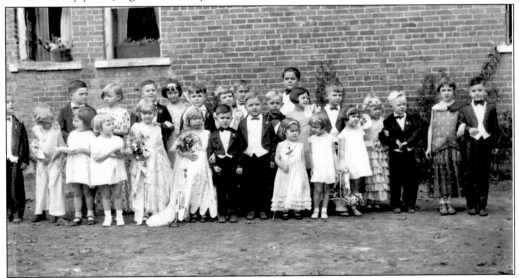

Twenty years later these miniature dramas were still a favorite Acworth event as is confirmed in this photograph of a 1931 Tom Thumb wedding. The wedding party includes young Acworthians Harrison, Durham, Winn, Adaway, Osborne, Patrick, McMillan, and Clark. (Robert M. Clark collection.)

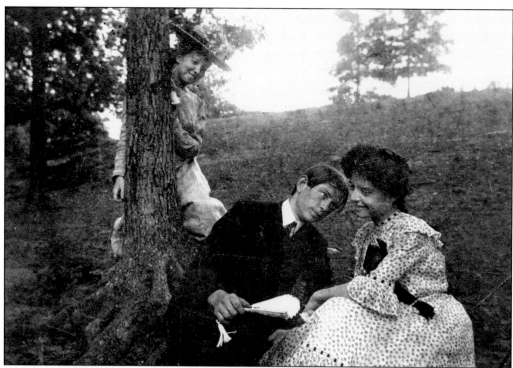

An admirer and her envious young friend join young Annie Lee Lemon, daughter of Jesse and Lizzie Lemon, in this early photograph. (Mark Lemon collection.)

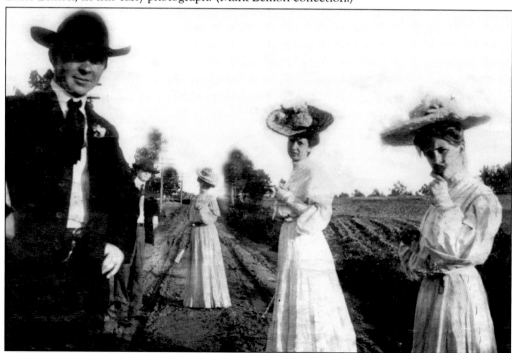

A handsome Acworth man has the attention of three local belles in this 1908 photograph. (Reginald Awtrey collection.)

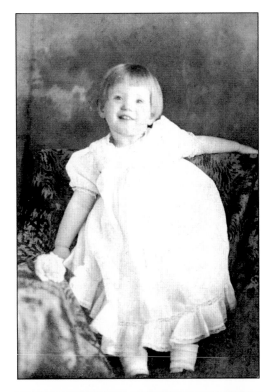

(*upper right*) Ernestine Collins Donahoo is a youngster in this studio photograph taken in the late 1920s. (McCoy family collection.)

(*bottom left*) Nancy Lee Smith Maxwell, age four, strikes a flirting pose for the photographer in this mid-1930s picture. (Nancy Smith Maxwell collection.)

(*bottom right*) The Fowler girls—Shirley, Beverly, and Jacqueline—pose in their party dresses in 1939. (Shirley Fowler Walker collection.)

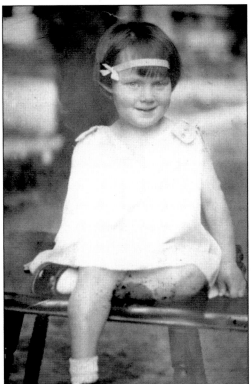

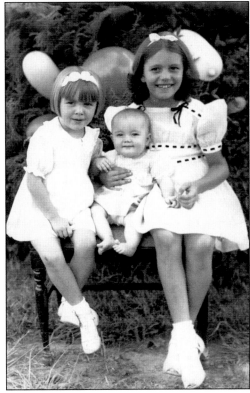

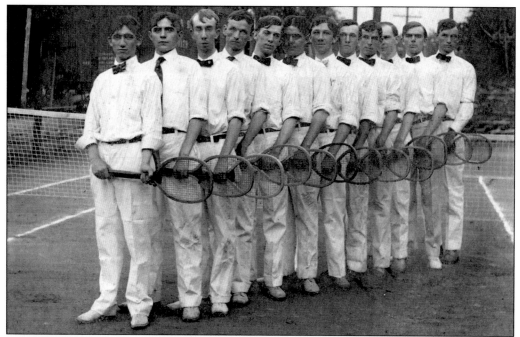

Tennis teams were an integral part of the sporting life in Acworth as is demonstrated by these nattily dressed teammates in a 1913 photograph. (Beth Watson collection.)

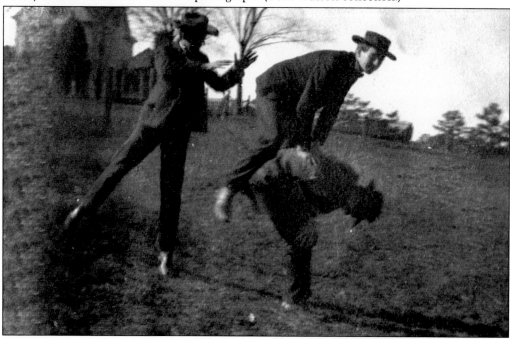

Unidentified young men play leapfrog behind the Awtrey homeplace. "Awtrey's Hill" included 75 acres—all the land behind the home bordered by Proctor Creek to the east, Dallas Street to the west, and the Terry dairy farm to the south (present-day Seminole Avenue). The large pasture was the site of children's play, picnics, and Confederate reunions. The City of Acworth baseball park was on the flattest part of the estate. (Reginald Awtrey collection.)

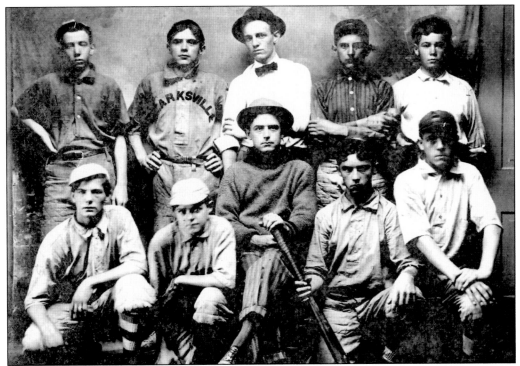

Baseball, a true American sport, has long been a part of life in Acworth as is obvious in this early 1900s photograph. Teammates are, from left to right, (front row) Paul McLain, Bay Lemon, Bob Lemon, Lewis McMillan, and Hilton Nichols; (back row) Roy Tippin, Bill Lemon, John Johnson, Ray Kemp, and Knox McMillan. (Willie B. Kemp collection.)

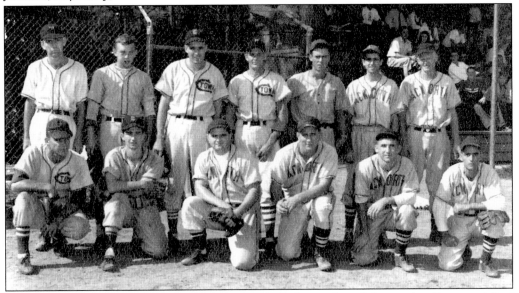

This late 1940s or early 1950s shot includes baseball players, from left to right, (front row) Red Stanley, Nebo Mitchell, Harold Harrison, Bill Casey, Ray Givan, and Robert Jones; (back row) Buddy Butler, Bobby Baker, James Owens, Frank Arp, Jimmy Ragsdale, Max Belcher, and Cotton Robertson. (Ben Flanagan collection.)

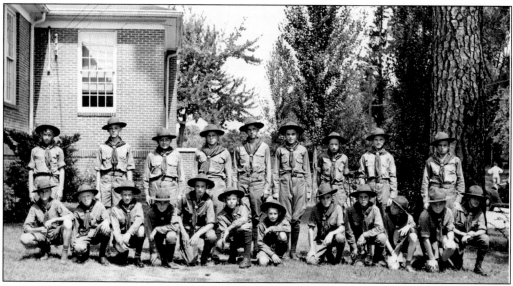

Since 1927, a mere 17 years after the founding of Boy Scouts of America, scouting activities have been an integral part of life for Acworth's youth. Troop 116 was originally chartered by Acworth United Methodist Church. The Optimist Club assumed sponsorship in the 1950s and 1960s; thereafter the charter returned to the Methodists' hands. In this 1930s photograph set to the backdrop of the new Acworth School, Acworth Scouts are decked out in their full uniform. (Willie B. Kemp collection.)

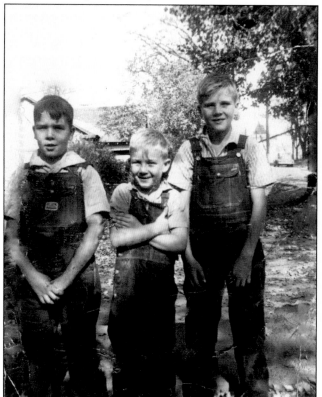

Dressed in overalls and fresh from working with Mr. Mitchell and Mr. Annis Fowler at the grist mill, young Hufstetler boys Edward, Billy, and Kenneth are shown in this 1940s photograph. Bill went on to a career in the Air Force and, over the years, Kenneth served the community as mayor, and Ed as a city alderman. (Elizabeth Hufstetler Craig collection.)

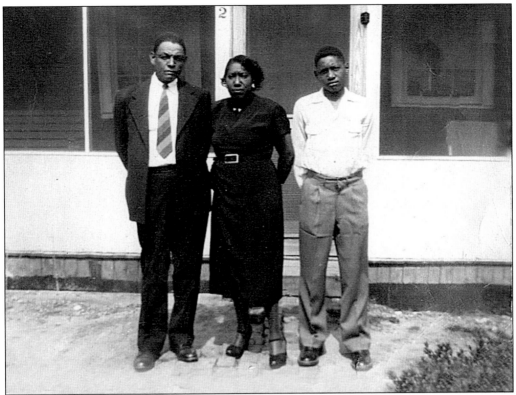

Pictured at the front door of their home in the late 1940s are Hillard, Henry, and Evelyn Gragg. Married in 1930, Hillard first worked in the ochre mines near Emerson. He then began a 20-year career with the railroad. Once her son was grown, Evelyn spent many years catering for local dinner parties and weddings and providing domestic services. Hillard was the son of Wiley Gragg. (Evelyn Gragg collection.)

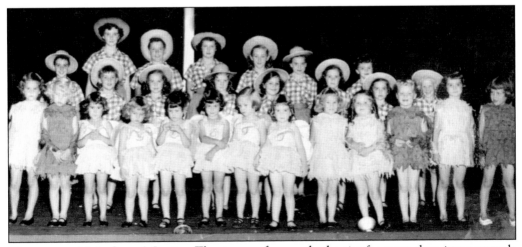

The stage at Main Street's Legion Theater was frequently the site for more than just newsreels and "moving picture" shows, as is shown in this early 1950s photograph of a dance recital. (Beth Watson collection.)

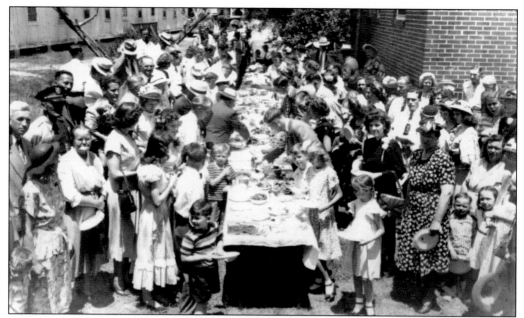

A large crowd of Acworthians gathers for fried chicken, potato salad, and homemade pies at an all-day singing and dinner on the grounds at Acworth School in the late 1940s. (Vanishing Georgia collection, Georgia Dept. of Archives and History.)

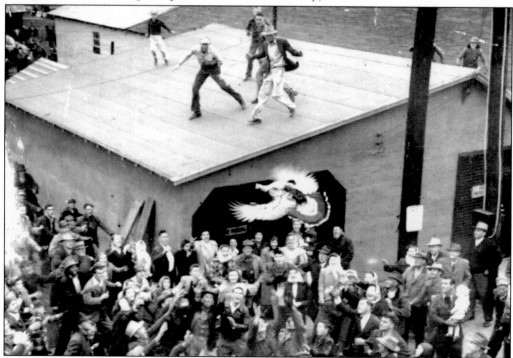

This 1950s photograph captures Acworthians enjoying a local holiday tradition, the "Turkey Trot." Annually, just prior to Christmas, 10 live turkeys were released from the rooftop of the city's fire station with this crowd responding enthusiastically. (Vanishing Georgia collection, Georgia Dept. of Archives and History.)

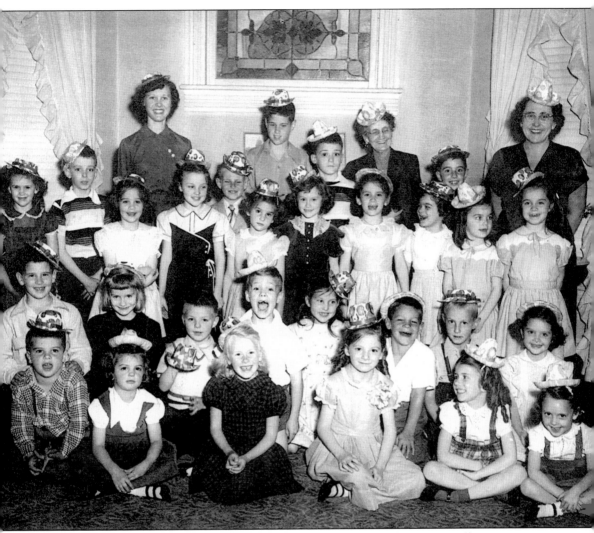

Young Sue McCall celebrates her birthday party with her friends at home on Collins Avenue in this 1950s photograph. Also in attendance were two especially prominent Acworth women. Fanny B. McClure (back left) had a deep and profound influence on Acworth youth, serving the community as a first-grade teacher for over 40 years. Her sister Charlotte also taught at Acworth and North Cobb High Schools. The McClure family owns property across from Mars Hill School. Mrs. Mary McCall (back right) nursed much of the community while assisting her husband, Dr. Moses McCall, during his many years in practice. A mother of six with a schedule full of PTA, church, and scouting activities, Mrs. McCall still found time to make her mark in the local political arena. First elected as city alderman in the fall of 1955, Mary went on to serve as the city's first female mayor from 1961 to 1966. (Beth Watson collection.)

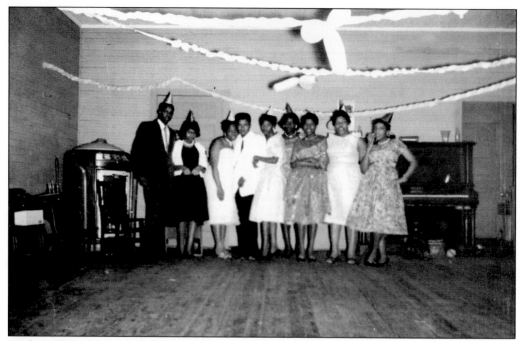

In the 1950s, crepe paper decorations and balloons adorned community gathering places all over town. Coupled with girls in pretty party dresses, local dances have long been a part of the Acworth social scene. (Tim Houston collection.)

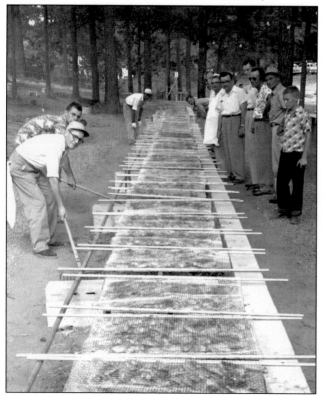

In the late 1930s under the financial pressures of the Great Depression, the Awtrey family was forced to develop their pastureland, and Seminole Drive became Acworth's first in-town subdivision. This photograph captures the barbeque that preceded the selling of the home lots by lottery. This barbecue tradition continued during the wartime years when families would spontaneously gather on an empty Seminole lot for impromptu picnics and cookouts. (Willie B. Kemp collection.)

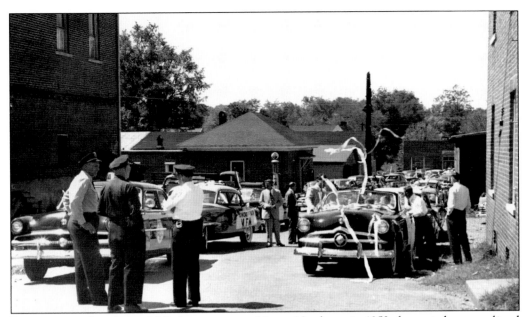

Prior to a parade to honor U.S. Army sergeant Vonne Newberry in 1953, decorated cars are lined up in front of the Masonic building, the jail, and city hall. A native son, Newberry was held for 33 months as a prisoner-of-war during the Korean Conflict. Upon his return to Acworth, the American Legion and city officials presented Vonne with a new Chevrolet. (Photo by Hollis Preast.)

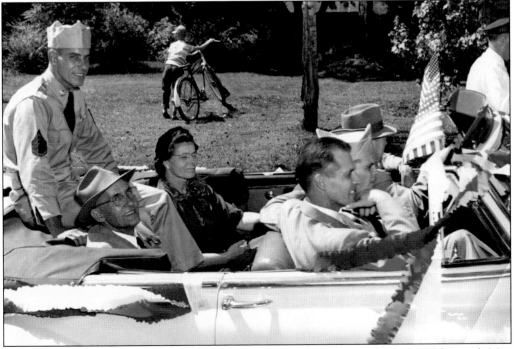

Newly released POW Vonne Newberry and his parents, James Walter "Walt" and Mae Newberry, are shown here on the ride through Acworth during a parade in his honor. (Photo by Hollis Preast.)

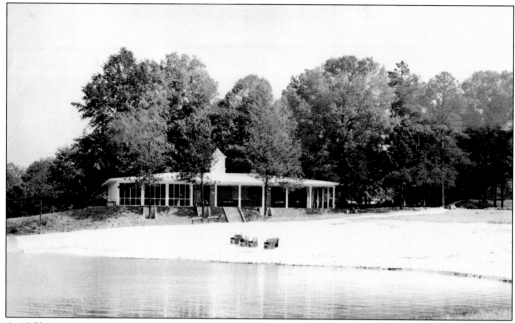

A 1953 "swimmers view" shows the Acworth Beach Bathhouse soon after its opening. (Photo by Hollis Preast.)

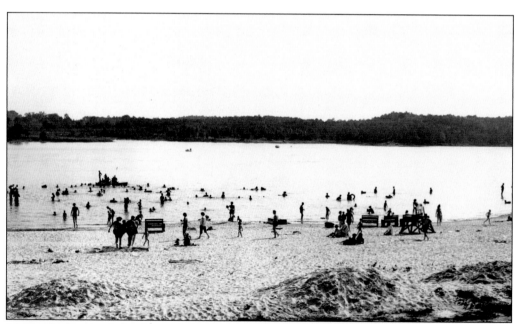

Large crowds enjoy Lake Acworth Beach long before the development of the northern shore of the lake. It is easy to see the small farms and undeveloped, heavily wooded areas where today Cobblestone Golf Course and home sites are located.

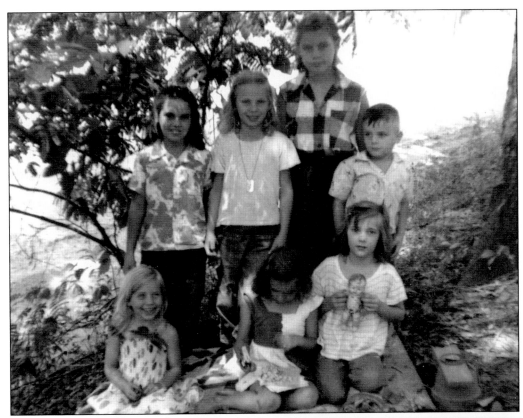

The Casey Gang, offspring of Bill and Mary Sue, are shown in this 1950s photograph enjoying a Sunday afternoon outing at the new Lake Acworth Beach. (Beth Watson collection.)

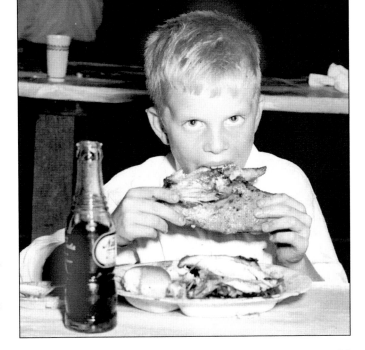

What better way to sum up small-town social events than this photograph of an unknown young Acworthian, enjoying fried chicken and a Nu Grape soda during the dedication celebration for the opening of Lake Acworth. (Photo by Joe McTyre.)

ENDNOTES

[1] Sarah Blackwell Gober Temple, *The First Hundred Years—A Short History of Cobb County in Georgia* (Cobb County, Ga.: Cobb Landmarks and Historical Society, 1997), p. 100.

[2] George White, *Statistics of the State of Georgia* (Savannah, Ga.: W. Thorne Williams, 1849), p. 188.

[3] Darlene R. Roth, Ph.D., *Architecture, Archaeology and Landscapes: Resources for Historic Preservation in Unincorporated Cobb County, Georgia* (Marietta, Georgia: Cobb County Historic Preservation Commission, 1988), p. 41.

[4] Carrie Dyer Woman's Club, *Acworth, Georgia from Cherokee County to Suburbia* (Acworth, Ga.: Star Printing, 1976), p. 17.

[5] "Acworth Section," *Marietta Daily Journal* (May 9, 1929), p. 49.

[6] Silena Jumper, *"Remember" The Georgia Removal, Trails Where They Cried."* (unpublished paper, 2002).

[7] Temple, p. 535.

[8] C.M. Gardner, Publisher, *The Marietta and Acworth City Directory 1883 and 1884*, (Gainesville, Ga.: Frank M. Pickrell, Printer, 1882).

[9] Civil War narration courtesy of Mark Lemon.

[10] Gardner.

[11] Dyer, pp. 64, 82.

[12] *Cobb County Times* (June 6 and June 13, 1935).

[13] Temple, p. 495.

[14] Dyer, p. 41.

[15] Ibid., p. 103.

[16] Ibid., pp. 35–37.

SOURCES

E.M. Bailey and Kate Good. *The Acworth Civic, Social, Cultural and Business Register 1860–1960.* (unpublished).

Carrie Dyer Woman's Club. *Acworth, Georgia from Cherokee County to Suburbia.* Acworth, Georgia: Star Printing, 1976.

C.M. Gardner, publisher. *The Marietta and Acworth City Directory 1883 and 1884.* Gainesville, Georgia: Frank M. Pickrell, Printer, 1882.

"Acworth Section." *Marietta Daily Journal.* May 9, 1929, pp. 49–56.

Cobb County Oral History Series. Kennesaw, Georgia: Kennesaw State University.

Darlene R. Roth, Ph.D. *Architecture, Archaeology and Landscapes: Resources for Historic Preservation in Unincorporated Cobb County, Georgia.* Marietta, Georgia: Cobb County Historic Preservation Commission, 1988.

Sarah Blackwell Gober Temple, *The First Hundred Years – A Short History of Cobb County in Georgia* (Cobb County, Ga.: Cobb Landmarks and Historical Society, 1997).

George White, *Statistics of the State of Georgia.* Savannah, Ga.: W. Thorne Williams, 1849.